INTERNATIONAL EXPRESS

Student's Book
Elementary

Liz Taylor and Alastair Lane

OXFORD
UNIVERSITY PRESS

OXFORD
UNIVERSITY PRESS

Great Clarendon Street, Oxford OX2 6DP

Oxford University Press is a department of the University of Oxford.
It furthers the University's objective of excellence in research, scholarship,
and education by publishing worldwide in

Oxford New York

Auckland Cape Town Dar es Salaam Hong Kong Karachi
Kuala Lumpur Madrid Melbourne Mexico City Nairobi
New Delhi Shanghai Taipei Toronto

With offices in

Argentina Austria Brazil Chile Czech Republic France Greece
Guatemala Hungary Italy Japan Poland Portugal Singapore
South Korea Switzerland Thailand Turkey Ukraine Vietnam

OXFORD and OXFORD ENGLISH are registered trade marks of
Oxford University Press in the UK and in certain other countries

© Oxford University Press 2007

The moral rights of the author have been asserted

Database right Oxford University Press (maker)

First published 2007

2012 2011 2010 2009 2008
10 9 8 7 6 5 4 3

No unauthorized photocopying

All rights reserved. No part of this publication may be reproduced,
stored in a retrieval system, or transmitted, in any form or by any means,
without the prior permission in writing of Oxford University Press,
or as expressly permitted by law, or under terms agreed with the appropriate
reprographics rights organization. Enquiries concerning reproduction
outside the scope of the above should be sent to the ELT Rights Department,
Oxford University Press, at the address above

You must not circulate this book in any other binding or cover
and you must impose this same condition on any acquirer

Any websites referred to in this publication are in the public domain and
their addresses are provided by Oxford University Press for information only.
Oxford University Press disclaims any responsibility for the content

ISBN: 978 0 19 456801 2

Printed in China

ACKNOWLEDGEMENTS

Illustrations by Fred Van Deelen/The Organisation pp 28-29; Mark Duffin pp 10, 11 (ruler) 18, 23, 30 (tickets), 46, 72-73; Dylan Gibson pp 19, 35, 55, 81, 89; Becky Halls/The Organisation pp 17, 27, 90; Martin Sanders pp 30 (map & signs), 31, 36, 40; Tony Sigley pp 11 (class), 24, 82-83, 91
We would also like to thank the following for permission to reproduce the following photographs: Cover images courtesy: RMI © Mango Productions/Corbis (girl at screen), RMI © Simon Marcus (man in airport lounge) and Alex Mares-Manton/Getty (girl in coffee bar), Alamy pp 43 (geothermal spa/Andrew Hasson), 44 (b/David Noton Photography), 47 (bananas/Foodfolio), (tea leaves/Aflo Foto Agency), 51 (a/Leo Himsl/FAN Travelstock), 59 (a/Paul Rapson), (b/Tomas del Amo), (c/Jim Wileman), (d/Stockfolio), 70 (Seoul/Alistair Ruff), 76 (SunnyPhotography.com), 78 (cell/Lisa Payne), 79 (Tracy Hallett), 85 (d/Chris Christodoulou/Lebrecht Music and Arts Photo Library), 86 (c/Blickwinkel), 87 (David Crausby); Corbis pp 6 (vineyards/John Miller/Robert Harding World Imagery), 36 (Steven Vidler/Eurasia Press), 44 (c/Gregor Schuster/Zefa), 45 (d/Dana Hoff), 48 (Michel Setboun), 50 (plane/George Hall), (train/Albrecht G. Schaefer), (Madrid, Warsaw & Budapest/Jon Hicks), (Bangkok/Steven Vidler/Eurasia Press), 56 (Jon Hicks), 60 (newsroom/Adrian Arbib), 62 (Tim Tadder), 84 (a/Adrian Wilson/Beateworks), (b/Carlos Dominguez), 88 (Handout/Scott Markowitz/Reuters); Getty Images pp 14 (bridge/Johner Images), 15 (Steve Murez/The Image Bank), 20 (Sean Justice/The Image Bank), 26 (Stewart Cohen/Stone), 37 (Justin Guariglia/National Geographic), 42 (Sakis Papadopoulos/The Image Bank), 43 (temple/Luis Veiga/The Image Bank), 51 (b/Southern Stock/Photonica), (c/Brian Bailey/Stone), 52 (Gallo Images-Emma Borg/The Image Bank), 57 (Altrendo Images), 60 (Kazuko/Peter Hendrie/Riser), 61 (university/Ron Krisel), (business trip/Ron Krisel), (travelling/John Cumming), 63 (Patti McConville), 64 (working late/Walter Hodges/Stone), 66 (woman/Hitoshi Nishimura), 68 (Seoul/Will & Deni McIntyre), 85 (c/Matthew Lewis/Stringer), 86 (a/David Trood), (b/Norbert Eisele-Hein/Look), (d/Zia Soleil/Iconica); Courtesy of Lonely Planet pp 32, 34; Lonely Planet Images p 68 (Warsaw/Krzysztof Dydynski); Courtesy of Jörgen Persson pp 14 (business card), 17, 22; PA Photos p 86 (Dean Karnazes/Mike Wintroath/AP); Photolibrary.com p 71; Punchstock pp 6 (Stephanie face on/David Woolley/Digital Vision), (Stephanie profile/David Woolley/Digital Vision), 7 (E Dygas/Digital Vision), 9 (Stephanie/David Woolley/Digital Vision), (Timo/Ryan McVay/Digital Vision), 12 (woman and two men/Allan Danahar/Digital Vision), 12 (three men/Jacobs Stock Photography/Digital Vision), (man and woman/Stockbyte), 13 (with screen/John Lund/Sam Diephuis/Digital Vision), (woman with glasses/Allan Danahar/Digital Vision), 16 (Stephanie/David Woolley/Digital Vision), (Timo/Ryan McVay/Digital Vision), 38 (LWA/Dann Tardif/Blend Images), 44 (a/Noel Hendrickson/Digital Vision), 47 (cup and teapot/Mixa Co. Ltd.), 61 (computer course/Glowimages), 64 (Marie/Digital Vision), 66 (man/Ryan McVay), 68 (man/Louis Fox/Digital Vision), (woman/Image Source), 70 (man/Louis Fox/Digital Vision), 86 (e/Digital Vision); Rex Features p 78 (room & lobby/Nigel R. Barklie)

Pictures sourced by Pictureresearch.co.uk

Sources

pp 86 – 88 http://www.thenorthface.com/na/our-story.html

Welcome

to International Express
Elementary Interactive Edition

Introduction There are ten units. Each unit begins with an *Agenda* which gives you details of the language you will study in the unit. This is followed by the three main parts: *Language focus*, *Wordpower*, and *Focus on communication*. There is a review unit after every two units.

Language focus First you meet new language, and have an opportunity to revise language you have already met. The new language is introduced through listening and reading texts. The texts are about topics of interest to professional people. You then look at how to form the language, the meaning, and how to use it. You discover rules about how the language works.

Practice
You practise using the language in a variety of situations: sometimes in speaking activities, sometimes in writing exercises. The activities and exercises help you to develop your ability to use the language and express yourself with confidence. You do some of the practice activities with another student or in a group.

Wordpower In the second part of the unit you meet new vocabulary and practise using it in speaking and writing activities. You also learn how to develop your vocabulary through word building and using collocations.

Focus on communication In the last part of each unit you learn the language you need for socializing and discussing work matters in meetings, on the telephone, and by email.

Review units There are five review units. You choose what to revise and complete the review exercises. You can use the Pocket Book for the areas that you need to review further.

Listening scripts and Answer key The scripts of all the listening material and the answers to the activities are available at the back of the book.

Pocket Book The Pocket Book (in the pouch at the back of the book) is divided into two sections, *Grammar* and *Functional English*. These summarize the key language points from the Student's Book. You can use the Pocket Book in your lessons or at work, and you can take it with you when you travel.

Multi-ROM The attached Multi-ROM has a selection of texts from the Student's Book accompanied by audio versions and dictations. These are linked to an interactive vocabulary list containing the key words and phrases from the book. There are also grammar and vocabulary practice activities.

Workbook There is an accompanying Workbook and Student's CD which have additional exercises on grammar, vocabulary, and functions, and give further practice in listening and pronunciation.

Good luck with learning English.

We hope you enjoy using *International Express*!

Contents

	Language focus	Wordpower	Focus on communication
1 Getting to know people			
p.6	• Present Simple (*I/you/we/they*) • Pronunciation: intonation of questions	• Classroom communication	• Introductions • Greetings and goodbyes
2 Lifestyles			
p.14	• Present Simple (*he/she/it*) • Adverbs of frequency • *love/like/enjoy* + *-ing* • Pronunciation: /s/ /z/ /ɪz/	• Time and numbers	• Starting a call ☎ • Time expressions
Review Unit A p.22			
3 Workplaces			
p.24	• *there is/there are* • *some/any* • *have, have got* • Pronunciation: linking	• Prepositions	• Asking for and giving directions • Asking for travel information
4 The road to success			
p.32	• Past Simple • Regular and irregular verbs • Pronunciation: /d/ /t/ /ɪd/ endings	• Travel for work	• Leaving a message ☎ • Telephone numbers ☎ • Spelling
Review Unit B p.40			
5 The world's largest industry			
p.42	• Mass and count nouns • *some, a lot of/much/many*	• Food file • Pronunciation: word stress • Using a dictionary	• Offers and requests • Eating and drinking • Pronunciation: sentence stress

	Language focus	Wordpower	Focus on communication
6 The best way to travel p.50	• Comparative and superlative adjectives	• Dates • Money • Pronunciation: /ð/ and /θ/	• Welcoming a visitor
Review Unit C p.58			
7 Life in the fast lane p.60	• Present Continuous • Present trends • Pronunciation: contracted forms in Present Continuous	• Word partners	• Making and changing arrangements
8 Relocating p.68	• Future: *will* • Future: *going to* • Pronunciation: contracted forms *'ll/won't*	• Communications file	• Writing emails and faxes
Review Unit D p.76			
9 Destination with a difference p.78	• Modal verbs: *should/shouldn't, may, can/can't, have to/don't have to* • Pronunciation: *can/can't*	• Hotel file	• Invitations • Suggestions
10 Developing a company p.86	• Past Simple and Present Perfect • Pronunciation: weak forms of *has/have*	• Verbs with prepositions	• Answerphone messages • Emails and mobile phones
Review Unit E p.94			
Listening scripts p.96			
Answer key p.103			

UNIT 1
Getting to know people

▼ AGENDA
▶ Present Simple (I/you/we/they)
▶ Classroom communication
▶ Introductions
▶ Greetings and goodbyes

Language focus

1 🎧 1.1 *Europa* magazine is about life in Europe today. Listen to the first part of an interview with Stephanie Debord for the magazine. Add the information to her profile.

★ **Europa** *Magazine* interviews Stephanie Debord

Profile
Name — Stephanie Debord
Country
Home town — Laforêt
Company — Legal Laforêt
Job — Lawyer
Married / Single
Children

2 Complete the sentences. Tell the class about yourself.

My name is …
I'm from …   (country)
I live in …   (place)
I work for …   (company/organization)
I'm a/an …   (job)
I'm …   (single/married)

3 🎧 1.1 Listen to the interview again. Complete the questions.

1 Where _____ _____ from?
2 Where _____ _____ live?
3 What _____ _____ do?
4 Which _____ do you work for?
5 _____ _____ single?

Work in pairs. Ask your partner the questions.

6 ● UNIT 1

4 Read about Timo Kekkonen's typical day. Complete the information about his day.

Timo Kekkonen

Hi. My name's Timo Kekkonen. I'm Finnish and I live in Espoo. I live with my partner, Seija. She's a receptionist at a hotel. We have a son, Matti. He's two. I work for a bank in Helsinki. I get up very early – at six o'clock, and I leave home at 6.30. I go to work by train. It takes an hour and it's very crowded. The normal time to start work at my company is eight o'clock. I get to work at 7.30 because I always have a lot of work. I finish work at 7 o'clock every day. I get home an hour later. It's a long day, but I don't work at the weekend.

A typical day	Timo	Stephanie
I get up at	6.00 (six o'clock)	7.15 (seven fifteen)
I leave home at		
I go to work by		
I get to work at		
I finish work at		
I get home at		

5 🎧 **1.2** Listen to the second part of the interview with Stephanie. Complete the information about her day in **4**.

Present Simple *I/you/we/they*

Read the examples and grammar rules.

Positive
I **live** in Laforêt.
I **go** to work by train.

Negative
I **don't work** at the weekend.
We **don't live** in Brussels.

Question
Do you **enjoy** your job?
Do you **get** home at 3.40?

Short answer
Yes, I do.
No, I don't.

- Use the Present Simple to talk about facts (e.g. *I live in Laforêt*) and regular activities (e.g. *I go to work by train*).
- Use *I/you/we/they* + infinitive (e.g. *enjoy*, *live*) to make positive sentences.
- Use *I/you/we/they* + *don't* (*do not*) + infinitive to make negative sentences.
- Use *Do* + *I/you/we/they* + infinitive to make *Yes/No* questions.

Correct the mistake.
Do you live in Milan? Yes, I live.

📗 *Pocket Book p. 11*

UNIT 1

> **Pronunciation**
>
> Look at the questions. We say them in different ways.
>
> a Do you come from Italy? ↗   b Where do you come from? ↘
>
> 🎧 **1.3 Listen and repeat.**
>
> 1 Are you Spanish?   6 Where do you live?
> 2 Is he a lawyer?   7 What do you do?
> 3 Do you come from Italy?   8 Where do you work?
> 4 Do you work in Rome?   9 How do you go to work?
> 5 Do you have any children? 10 What time do you get home?

Practice

1 Put the words in the correct order to make the interviewer's questions.

1 you/get up/do/what time?   *What time do you get up?*
2 do/leave/you/what time/home?   _____
3 go/how/you/do/to work?   _____
4 get/what time/to work/you/do?   _____
5 finish/do/what time/work/you?   _____
6 home/what time/you/do/get?   _____

2 Work in pairs. Ask your partner the questions in **1**. Answer your partner's questions.

3 Are any of your answers the same as your partner's answers? Tell the class.
Example *We both start work at 8 o'clock.*

4 🎧 **1.4** Listen to Stephanie and Timo talking about their jobs. Tick (✓) the things they do.

At work	Stephanie	Timo	You
I read and write emails.	☐	☐	☐
I read financial newspapers.	☐	☐	☐
I look at information on the Internet.	☐	☐	☐
I make phone calls.	☐	☐	☐
I have meetings with clients and customers.	☐	☐	☐
I give advice/information.	☐	☐	☐
I have meetings with colleagues.	☐	☐	☐
I have business lunches.	☐	☐	☐
I travel to other cities/countries.	☐	☐	☐

5 Tick (✓) the things you do in **4**. What other things do you do? Tell the class about your working day or a day of study.

6 Read what Stephanie and Timo say about using English in their jobs. What do they find difficult?

Europa Magazine

Business Language

Stephanie Debord

I'm a lawyer in the south of Belgium and my clients work in agriculture. They do business with countries like the UK and the USA. They get a lot of documents in English. So I read and explain the documents for them. I don't speak much English at work. I sometimes answer the phone, but it's difficult to understand. I prefer using English for emails and letters.

Timo Kekkonen

English is very important in my job. All the information I need is in English. My colleagues are in the USA. We speak on the phone and write emails in English. I use English all the time – speaking English is a normal part of my life. I love speaking English and working with people from other countries. It's great. But when I write emails in English I make a lot of spelling mistakes. It's really tricky!

7 Work in groups. Why do you need English? Make a list. Present your list to the class.

Examples

We	need English for	our jobs.
		work in the future.
		travel.

We	need English to	speak on the phone.
		read and write emails.

UNIT 1 9

Wordpower

Classroom communication

1 Complete the questions with a verb from the box.

| excuse | borrow | understand | spell ✓ | mean |
| say (x 2) | write | repeat | speak | |

1 How do you __spell__ *colleague*?
2 Sorry, can you _____ the question?
3 _____ me, can you _____ that again, please?
4 Can you _____ slowly, please?
5 How do you _____ *autostrada* in English, please?
6 Can you _____ the word on the board, please?
7 Can I _____ your dictionary, please?
8 What does the word *leisure* _____?
9 What's the word for this in English?
10 I'm sorry, I don't _____.

2 🎧 **1.5** Listen to a teacher and some students. It is the first lesson of an English course. Match the students to the departments.

1 Menno   a Marketing
2 William   b Reception
3 Evelyn   c Accounts

3 This is the office where Alice and the students have the English lesson. Match the words and pictures a–k.

a dictionary   an eraser   a hole punch   a paper clip
a folder   a pen   a pencil   a whiteboard   a piece of paper
a laptop   a notebook

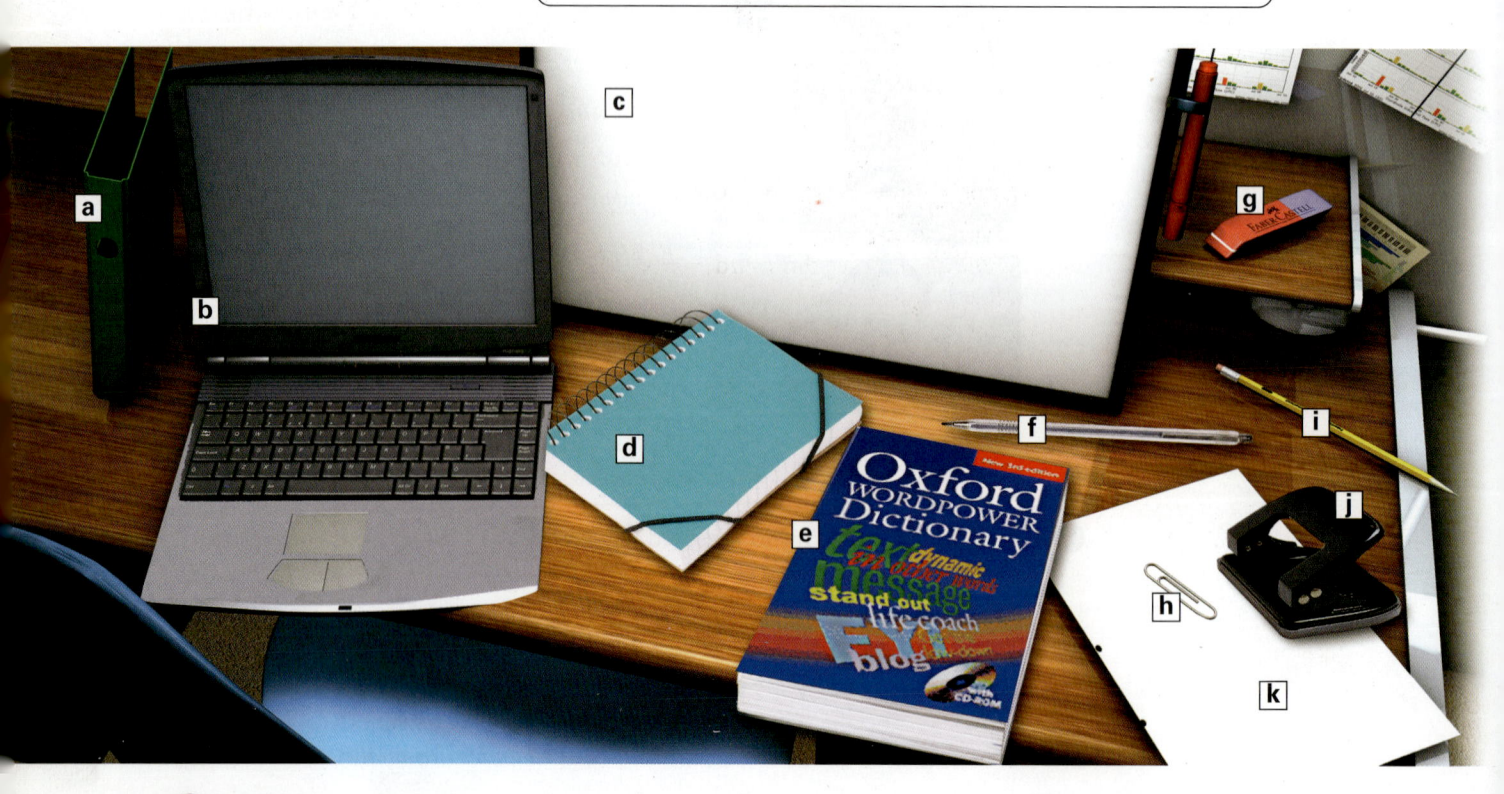

10 UNIT 1

4 🎧 **1.6** Alice and the students continue the lesson. Listen and answer the questions.

1 Can they use a whiteboard in the lesson?
2 Do they use a CD player?

5 Work in pairs. Look at the words in **3**. Do you have the things in the classroom today? Ask your partner.

Example Student A *Do you have an eraser?*
Student B *Yes, I do.*

6 Give the English word for other things in your classroom. Ask your teacher if you don't know the English word.

7 Work in pairs: Student A and Student B. Ask and answer questions using the role cards below.

STUDENT A

Ask Student B these five questions.

Can you speak more slowly, please?

Can I borrow a dictionary, please?

How do you spell *eraser*?

Do you have a CD player?

What's the word for this in English?

Here are the answers to Student B's questions. Choose the correct answer.

1 It's d-i-c-t-i-o-n-a-r-y.
2 Text message.
3 Yes. No problem.
4 It's a thing that teachers write on in the classroom.
5 Sorry, I only have one.

STUDENT B

Here are the answers to Student A's questions. Choose the correct answer.

1 Here you are. It's English-German.
2 Ruler.
3 Yes, it's behind you.
4 Sorry. I speak very fast.
5 It's e-r-a-s-e-r.

Ask Student A these five questions.

How do you say *SMS* in English?

What is a whiteboard?

How do you spell *dictionary*?

Can I borrow a pen?

Can we have the lesson in my office?

8 Here are some classroom problems. Match comments 1–4 with pictures a–d.

1 Sorry, I can't hear.
2 Sorry, I can't see the board.
3 Sorry, I can't read the sentence.
4 Sorry, I don't know the answer.

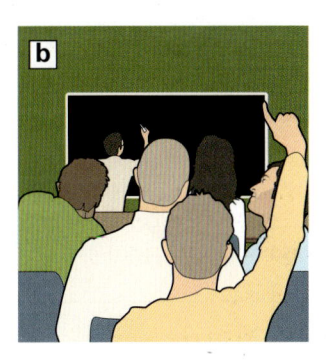

9 All the sentences in **8** start with *sorry*. Do you use *sorry* a lot in your language?

UNIT 1 11

Focus on communication

Introductions

1 Look at the pictures. What are the people saying?

2 🎧 **1.7** Listen to three conversations. Match the conversations to the pictures.
Conversation 1 ☐ 2 ☐ 3 ☐

3 🎧 **1.7** Listen again and complete the conversations.

Conversation 1

A Dieter, _can I introduce you to_ [1] José Corra? José, _____ [2] Dieter Hann.

B Pleased to meet you.

C _____ [3].

A José is the manager at our office in Barcelona.

Conversation 2

A _____ [4] myself? _____ [5] is Pietro Zenari.

B Hello. Nice to meet you. I'm Jackie Pons.

Conversation 3

A Lisa, _____ [6] Marcel Tullier? Marcel, _____ [7] a colleague of mine, Lisa White.

B _____ [8], Lisa. _____ [9].

C Hi, nice to meet you too, Marcel.

4 Work in groups. Practise the conversations in **3**.

Greetings and goodbyes

1 Match the phrase with the explanation.

We say

1 *Good morning* ☐   a after about 6 o'clock
2 *Good afternoon* ☐   b before we go to bed
3 *Good evening* ☐   c all morning, until lunch time
4 *Good night* ☐   d from after lunch until about 6 o'clock

2 🎧 **1.8** Listen to four conversations. Match two of the conversations to the pictures.

Picture a   Conversation ☐
Picture b   Conversation ☐

3 🎧 **1.8** Listen to the conversations again. Tick (✓) the phrases you hear.

Greetings

Good morning/afternoon/evening. ☐	
Hello … ☐	
Hi … ☐	
It's good to see you again. ☐	It's nice to be here again. ☐
How are you? ☐	Very well, thanks. And you? ☐
How's the family? ☐	Fine, thanks. ☐
How's everything? ☐	

Goodbyes

It was nice meeting you. ☐	I enjoyed meeting you, too. ☐
It was great seeing you. ☐	
Have a good trip. ☐	
I hope to see you again soon. ☐	
See you again soon. ☐	
Goodbye. ☐	
Bye. ☐	

📘 Pocket Book p.14

4 Walk around the class. Practise greeting and saying goodbye to the other students. Use the phrases in **3**.

- greet someone you know
- introduce yourself to someone you don't know
- say goodbye

UNIT 1

UNIT 2
Lifestyles

▼ **AGENDA**
- Present Simple (*he/she/it*)
- Adverbs of frequency
- *love/like/enjoy* + *-ing*
- Time and numbers
- Starting a call
- Time expressions

Language focus 1

1 Read the article *Across the bridge* and answer the questions.
1 How long does Jörgen spend travelling every day?
2 How does he travel?
3 Does he have a long lunch break?

*Europa*Magazine

Across the bridge

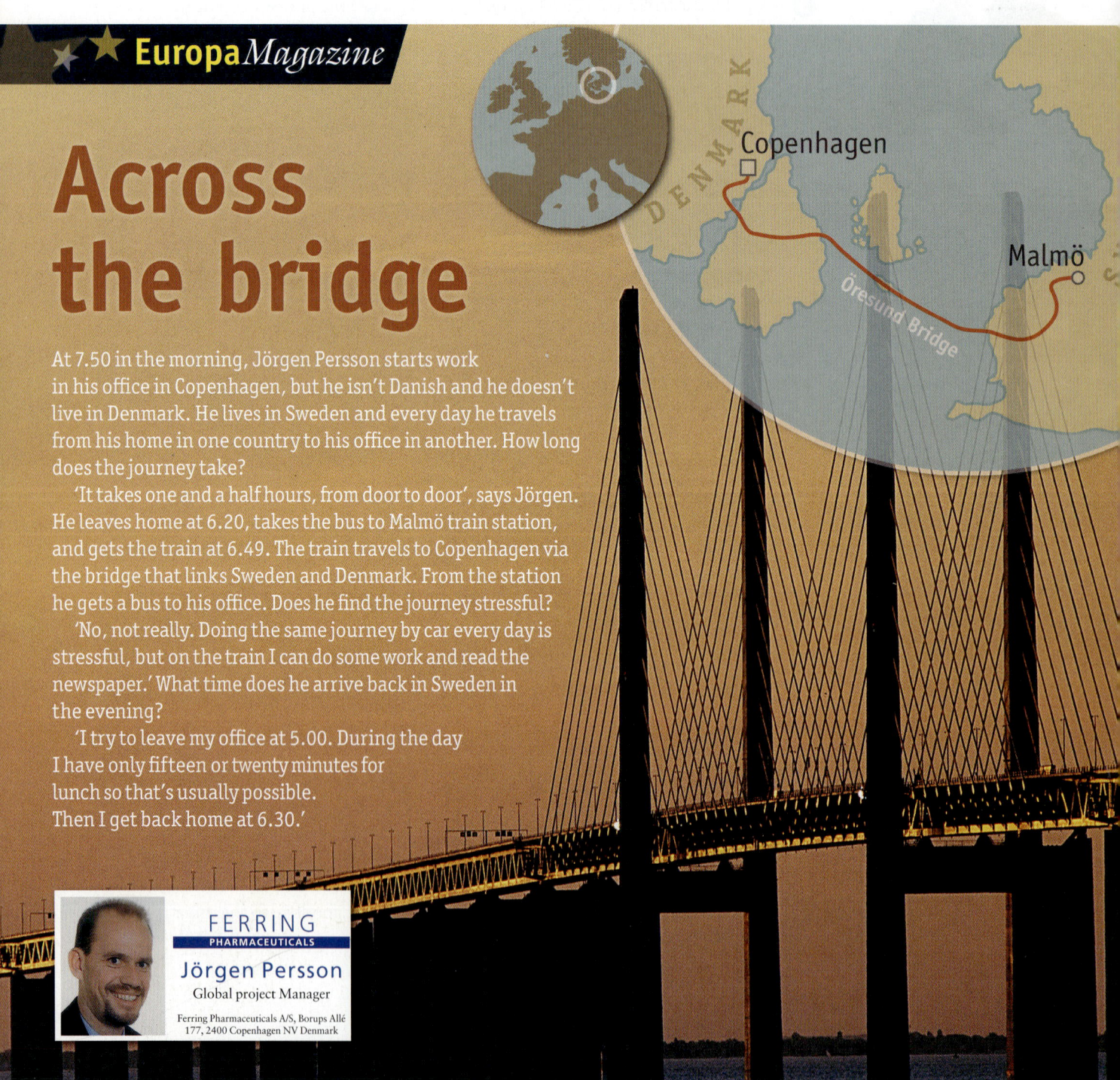

At 7.50 in the morning, Jörgen Persson starts work in his office in Copenhagen, but he isn't Danish and he doesn't live in Denmark. He lives in Sweden and every day he travels from his home in one country to his office in another. How long does the journey take?

'It takes one and a half hours, from door to door', says Jörgen. He leaves home at 6.20, takes the bus to Malmö train station, and gets the train at 6.49. The train travels to Copenhagen via the bridge that links Sweden and Denmark. From the station he gets a bus to his office. Does he find the journey stressful?

'No, not really. Doing the same journey by car every day is stressful, but on the train I can do some work and read the newspaper.' What time does he arrive back in Sweden in the evening?

'I try to leave my office at 5.00. During the day I have only fifteen or twenty minutes for lunch so that's usually possible. Then I get back home at 6.30.'

FERRING PHARMACEUTICALS
Jörgen Persson
Global project Manager
Ferring Pharmaceuticals A/S, Borups Allé 177, 2400 Copenhagen NV Denmark

Present Simple *he/she/it*

Read the examples and grammar rules.

Positive
- He **leaves** home at 6.20.
- His journey **takes** one and a half hours.

Negative
- He **doesn't live** in Denmark.

Question
- **Does** he **work** on the train?
- **Does** he **have** a long lunch break?

Short answer
Yes, he **does**.
No, he **doesn't**.

Question
- How long **does** the journey **take**?
- What time **does** he **arrive** back in Sweden?

Answer
It **takes** an hour and a half.
He **arrives** back at 6.30.

Note *doesn't = does not*

- Use the Present Simple to talk about routine activities and facts.
- The positive form always ends in *-s*.
- To make the negative use *doesn't* (*does not*) + infinitive (e.g. *study, leave*).
- To make the question use *does* + *he/she/it* + infinitive.

Correct the mistakes.
1 She start work at 8.30
2 He doesn't lives here.
3 Does it arrives every day?

Pocket Book p.11

Pronunciation

Look at the verb endings. We say them in different ways. What is the difference?

live   lives
start   starts
finish finishes

🎧 2.1 Write *lives*, *starts*, and *finishes* in the correct column. Then listen and repeat.

/s/	/z/	/ɪz/
____	____	____
works	does	discusses
gets	arrives	watches
speaks	travels	studies
makes	leaves	

Practice ① Complete the description of Karin Fisch. Use the correct form of the verb in brackets.

Karin Fisch ___comes___ (come) from Germany. She _____¹ (live) in Hamburg and _____² (work) for a company which _____³ (develop) computer software. She _____⁴ (go) to work by car and _____⁵ (start) work at 8.00. At work she _____⁶ (not, have) time for lunch, so she usually _____⁷ (eat) a sandwich at her desk. She _____⁸ (work) late so she _____⁹ (not, go out) a lot in the evenings. Her hobby _____¹⁰ (be) painting. She _____¹¹ (paint) landscapes and she _____¹² (have) exhibitions of her paintings in Hamburg.

2 Make questions about Karin.

1 Where/come from?   *Where does she come from?*
2 live/in Hamburg?
3 work/for a bank?
4 How/go to work?
5 What time/start/work?
6 What/eat/for lunch?
7 go out a lot/in the evenings?
8 What/paint?
9 Where/have/exhibitions?

3 Work in pairs. Ask and answer the questions in **2**. The answers are in **1**.

Example *Does she live in Hamburg?*
Yes, she does.

Language focus 2

1 🎧 **2.2** Listen to Stephanie and Timo. Tick (✓) the things they do in the evening and at weekends.

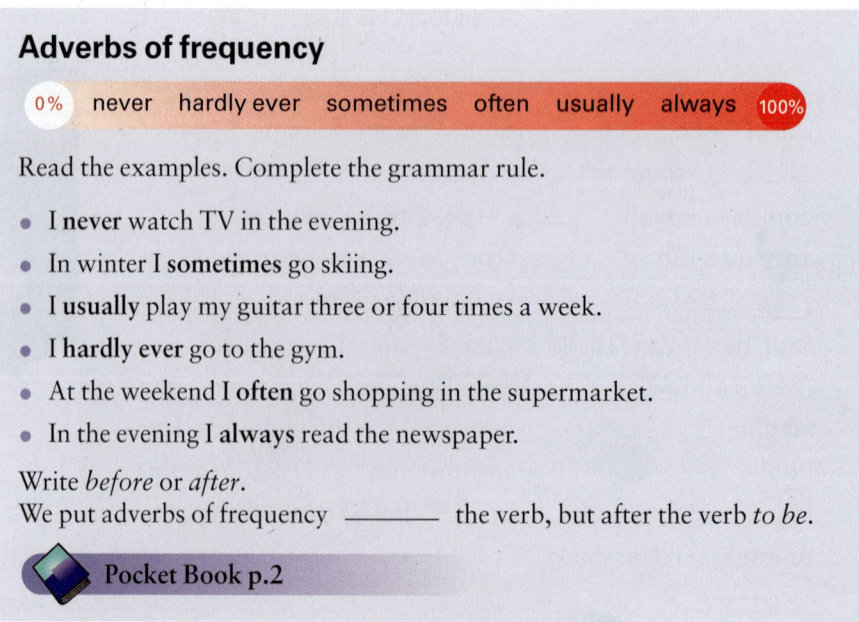

Evening and weekend activities	Stephanie	Timo
watch TV		
relax		
go shopping		
read		
play the guitar		
go cycling	✓	
go swimming		
go skiing		
invite friends		
have parties		

Adverbs of frequency

0%   never   hardly ever   sometimes   often   usually   always   100%

Read the examples. Complete the grammar rule.

- I **never** watch TV in the evening.
- In winter I **sometimes** go skiing.
- I **usually** play my guitar three or four times a week.
- I **hardly ever** go to the gym.
- At the weekend I **often** go shopping in the supermarket.
- In the evening I **always** read the newspaper.

Write *before* or *after*.
We put adverbs of frequency _____ the verb, but after the verb *to be*.

📘 Pocket Book p.2

16 ● UNIT 2

Practice

1 Work in pairs. Tell your partner which of the activities in **Language Focus 2** you do, and how often you do them. Use *always/often/sometimes*, etc.

Example *At the weekend I often go shopping in the supermarket.*

2 Tell the class about your partner.

Example *My partner sometimes goes cycling.*

3 Work in pairs. Match the activities and pictures a–j.

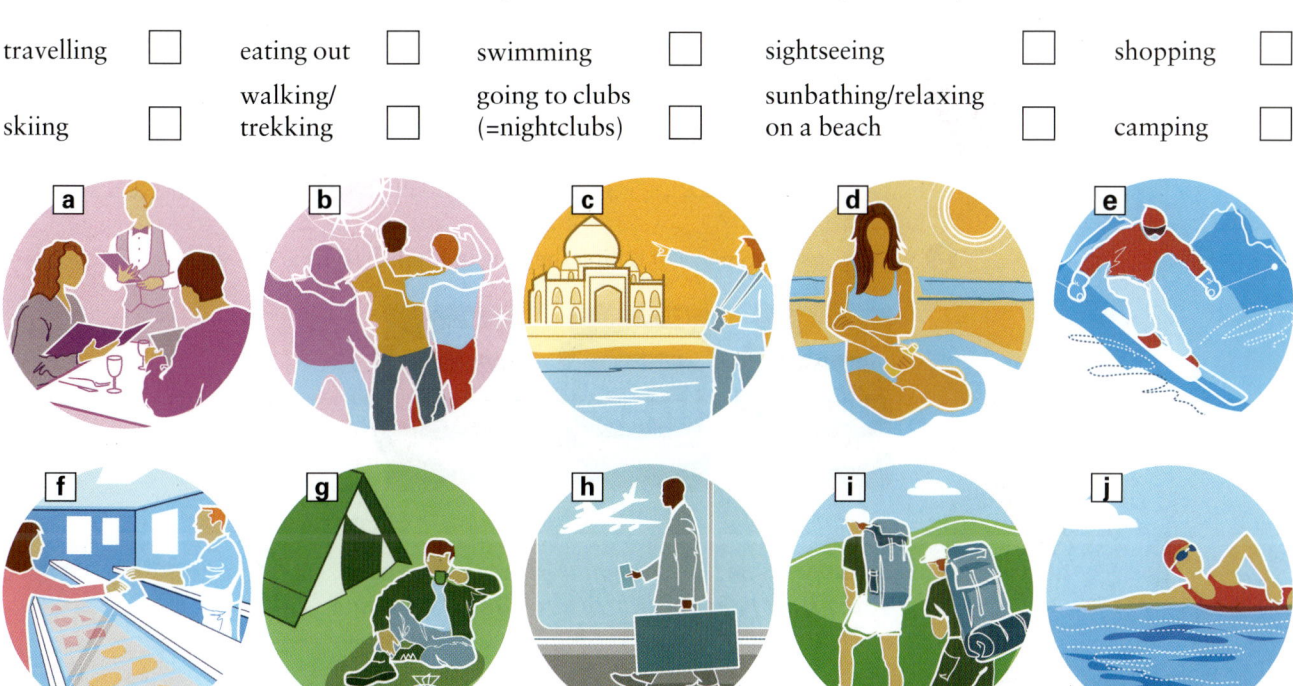

| travelling ☐ | eating out ☐ | swimming ☐ | sightseeing ☐ | shopping ☐ |
| skiing ☐ | walking/trekking ☐ | going to clubs (=nightclubs) ☐ | sunbathing/relaxing on a beach ☐ | camping ☐ |

4 🎧 **2.3** Listen and read what Jörgen likes doing on holiday.

'What kind of holidays do I enjoy? Well, I really enjoy travelling to new places. I like lots of activity when I'm on holiday. I love walking and trekking – my next holiday is trekking in the jungle in Thailand. I don't enjoy doing nothing when I'm on holiday. For example, I don't like lying on a beach. OK, sometimes, when I'm very tired, I can relax on a beach for two days, but then I'm ready for something active again!'

5 What things does Jörgen enjoy doing on holiday? What things does he not enjoy?

6 What form of the verb do we use after *enjoy*, *like*, and *love*?

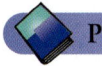

Pocket Book p.5

7 Work in pairs. Find out which activities your partner likes doing on holiday.

Ask   *Do you like/enjoy …?*
Answer   *Yes, I do./No, I don't.*

8 Tell the class what your partner likes doing on holiday.

UNIT 2   17

Wordpower

Time and numbers

❶ 🎧 2.4 Listen to the examples.

a 13 thirteen   b 30 thirty

❷ 🎧 2.5 Underline the number you hear.
1 <u>14</u> 40   3 17 70
2 16 60   4 18 80

❸ Work in pairs. In turns say all the numbers in ❷.

❹ 🎧 2.6 Write the numbers you hear.
1 _43_   2 ___   3 ___   4 ___   5 ___   6 ___

❺ There are two ways of telling the time in English. One is this way.

We say
eight thirty a.m.   or   *eight thirty in the morning*
three fifteen p.m.   or   *three fifteen in the afternoon*
seven fifty p.m.   or   *seven fifty in the evening*

❻ 🎧 2.7 Listen to the examples.

❼ This is the second way of telling the time. Look at the clock.

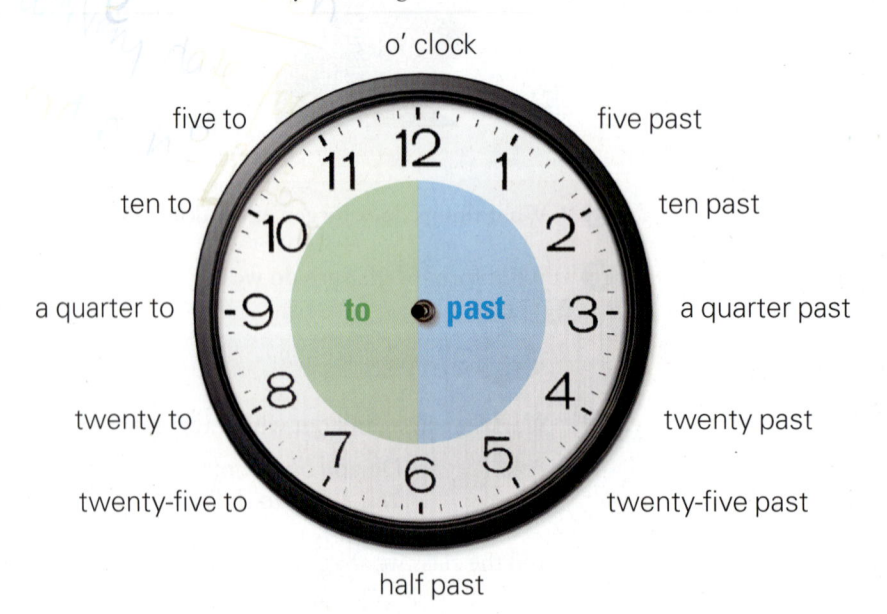

o' clock
five to — five past
ten to — ten past
a quarter to — a quarter past
twenty to — twenty past
twenty-five to — twenty-five past
half past

❽ Look again at the clocks in ❺ and ❻. Tell the time using the words from ❼.

18 UNIT 2

9 Work in pairs. Play the game, 'Ricardo's day'. Use the verbs in the box to help you.

> have a coffee break   eat lunch   visit the factory   speak with his boss
> get to work   catch the bus   have another coffee break   check his diary
> deal with the paperwork   leave work   get home   attend a meeting

Toss a coin.
Heads = move one square.
Tails = move two squares.

On each square, say the time and say what Ricardo does every day at the time.

Example: He catches the bus at quarter past seven.

The person who arrives on the finish square first is the winner.

UNIT 2   19

Focus on communication

Starting a call

1 Do you know any typical telephone phrases? What do you say when you:
- give your name?
- ask to speak to someone?

2 Read the telephone conversation. We do not use the underlined phrases on the telephone. What do we say?

RECEPTIONIST   Good morning. L. S. Communications.
MARIO   Good morning. <u>I want</u> Anna Pilon, please.
RECEPTIONIST   <u>Wait</u>, please.
ANNA   Hello.
MARIO   Hello. <u>Are you</u> Anna Pilon?
ANNA   <u>Yes, I am</u>.
MARIO   <u>I'm</u> Mario Bardo. <u>I call</u> about …

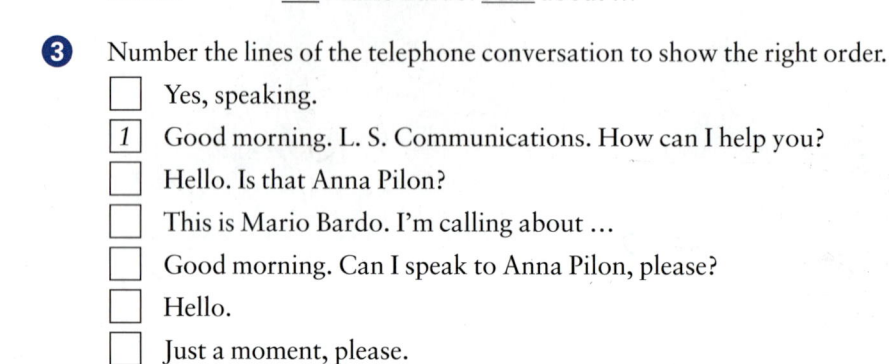

3 Number the lines of the telephone conversation to show the right order.

☐ Yes, speaking.
[1] Good morning. L. S. Communications. How can I help you?
☐ Hello. Is that Anna Pilon?
☐ This is Mario Bardo. I'm calling about …
☐ Good morning. Can I speak to Anna Pilon, please?
☐ Hello.
☐ Just a moment, please.

4 🎧 2.8 Listen and check your answers.

5 Write the typical telephone phrases from the conversation in **3** for:

1 I want   _Can I speak to_   4 Yes, I am. _____
2 Wait   _____   5 I'm   _____
3 Are you   _____   6 I call   _____

6 Practise the conversation in **3** in pairs. Change roles and practise again.

7 Read the telephone conversation below. The missing phrases are in the box on the left. Write the letter in the space.

RECEPTIONIST   AMC Design. _d_ ¹?
PETE   Oh, hello. _____² Jon Dunn, please?
RECEPTIONIST   _____³
PETE   _____⁴ Pete May from Novac.
RECEPTIONIST   _____⁵
JON   Hello, Pete. It's Jon. How are you?
PETE   Fine, thanks, Jon. _____⁶ our next meeting. Are you free on Thursday afternoon, at 4 o'clock?

a It's …
b Could I speak to …?
c I'm phoning about …
d How can I help you? ✓
e Who's calling, please?
f Hold on, please.

8 🎧 2.9 Listen and check your answers.

Write the phrases with the same meaning from **7**.

Can I speak to … ?   Just a moment, please.   I'm calling about …
_____   _____   _____

Pocket Book p.17

20 UNIT 2

9 Work in pairs. Practise starting a call. Use phrases from **7**. Then change roles and practise again.

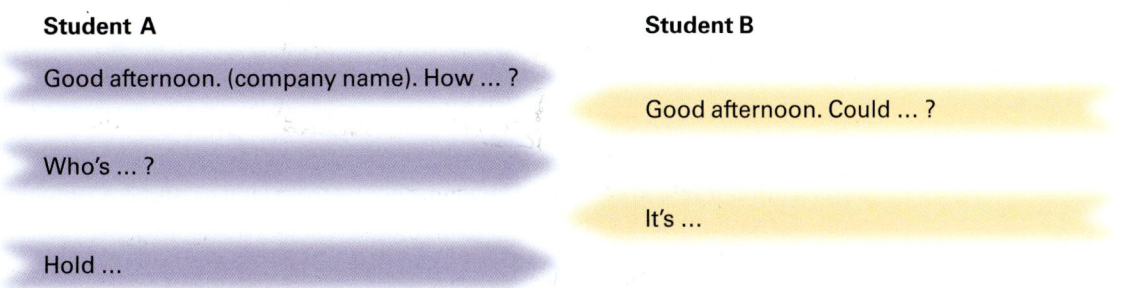

Student A
- Good afternoon. (company name). How … ?
- Who's … ?
- Hold …

Student B
- Good afternoon. Could … ?
- It's …

Time expressions

1 Read these emails. Underline the time expressions.

Email 1
To: j.dunn@global.net
Subject: Meeting next week

Jon
Can we get together for a meeting on Monday, at 4 p.m., if that's possible? If not, how about on Tuesday, in the afternoon, or if you prefer, at midday?
Regards
Pete

Email 2
To: mayp@novac.com
Subject: Meeting next week

Sorry, next Monday isn't possible but I can make it on Tuesday afternoon at 3 o'clock, if that's OK with you.
Regards
Jon

Email 3
To: j.osti@hotmail.com
Subject: Translations

Dear Judy
Many thanks for your help last week. My client was on the phone yesterday evening asking for the translations. Can you email them to me tomorrow morning?
Best wishes
Anna Perini

2 Work in pairs. Write the time expressions in the table.

at	on	in	no preposition	
11.15 a.m.	_Monday_	the morning	next weekend	yesterday
____	Wednesday morning	____	____	____ afternoon
____	____	the evening	last month	tomorrow
the weekend	Thursday evening		year	

3 Complete the email with the correct preposition *at*, *on*, *in*, or leave with no preposition.

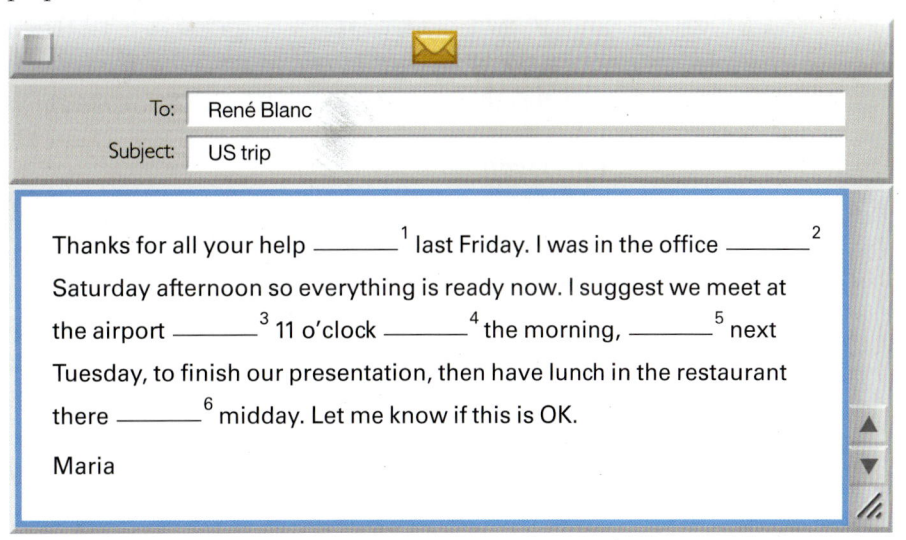

To: René Blanc
Subject: US trip

Thanks for all your help ____¹ last Friday. I was in the office ____² Saturday afternoon so everything is ready now. I suggest we meet at the airport ____³ 11 o'clock ____⁴ the morning, ____⁵ next Tuesday, to finish our presentation, then have lunch in the restaurant there ____⁶ midday. Let me know if this is OK.

Maria

UNIT 2   21

REVIEW UNIT A

▼ AGENDA
- Grammar ❶, ❷, ❹, ❺
- Vocabulary ❸, ❻
- Communication ❼–❾

This unit reviews the main language points from Units 1 and 2. Complete the exercises. Check your learning with the self-check box at the end.

❶ Present Simple

Complete the description. Write the correct form of the verb in brackets.

Jörgen Persson _____¹ (speak) three languages at work every day – Swedish, Danish, and English. At the company's head office in Copenhagen there _____² (be) people of fifteen different nationalities and they all _____³ (communicate) in English. Jörgen also _____⁴ (use) English when he _____⁵ (travel) to different countries and _____⁶ (visit) other Ferring companies. He _____⁷ (do) a lot of travelling and _____⁸ (go) to international congresses in the autumn. He _____⁹ (be) away from home fifty per cent of the time then, and often _____¹⁰ (work) at weekends, too.

❷ Present Simple

Write the questions.

1 Where/they/live? _____
2 Who/he/work for? _____
3 she/go to work/by car? _____
4 What time/you/start work? _____
5 What/she/do/in her job? _____
6 you/use/English at work? _____

❸ Vocabulary: word pairs

Match verbs in A with nouns in B to make word pairs.

Example *give advice*

A			B		
have	write	visit	emails	clients	newspapers
give ✓	go	watch	shopping	advice ✓	English on the phone
speak	read		time	TV	

❹ Frequency adverbs

Write five true sentences about yourself. Use word pairs from ❸ and frequency adverbs (*always, usually, often, sometimes, hardly ever, never*).

Example *I sometimes speak English on the phone.*

❺ love/like/enjoy + -ing

Work in pairs. Ask your partner questions about these activities. Then complete the sentences.

Example *Do you enjoy dancing?*

cycling	skiing	getting up early	watching TV
going for walks	sunbathing	swimming	studying for exams
learning English	going to clubs	sightseeing	playing computer games

My partner
1 loves …   2 likes …   3 enjoys …   4 doesn't like …   5 doesn't enjoy …

22 ● REVIEW UNIT A

6 Time

Work in pairs. Say the times.

09:15   10:30   02:45   06:50

7 Introductions, greetings and goodbyes

Work in pairs. What do you reply?

1 Pleased to meet you.
2 Nice to meet you.
3 It's good to see you again.
4 How's everything?
5 How are you?
6 How's the family?
7 It was nice meeting you.
8 Have a good trip.

8 Telephoning

Complete the telephone conversation. Write one word in each gap.

A Good morning. Radfords. How _____ _____ _____ [1] you?
B Good morning. _____ _____ _____ [2] to Matt Hudson, please?
A Who's _____ [3], please?
B Emma Hite, from Infosystems.
A _____ [4] on, please.
C Hello.
B Hello. Is _____ [5] Matt Hudson?
C Yes, _____ [6].
B _____ _____ [7] Emma Hite. I'm _____ [8] about your computer problem …

9 Time expressions

Write the words in the correct group.

midday ✓	the afternoon	next year	Tuesday evening
10.30 a.m.	the weekend	the morning	Sunday morning
next Saturday	last weekend	4 o'clock	yesterday morning
Wednesday	the evening		

at	on	in	no preposition
midday			

Look at the self-check box. Tick the areas you need to review again.

SELF-CHECK BOX	Yes	No	Pocket Book
• Present Simple			11
• Frequency adverbs			2
• *love, like, enjoy* + *-ing*			5
• Vocabulary: word pairs			
• Time			
• Introductions, greetings, goodbyes			14
• Telephoning			17
• Time expressions			

REVIEW UNIT A

UNIT 3
Workplaces

▼ **AGENDA**
- there is/there are
- some/any
- have, have got
- Prepositions
- Asking for and giving directions
- Asking for travel information

Language focus

1 Look at the picture. It shows the office of Force Architects. Match the descriptions 1–6 with the rooms a–f.

1 Eva's office has a large desk and pictures of modern buildings on the walls. She's got a laptop. There aren't any books.

2 Yuri is responsible for the company website and the computer system. He's got lots of computers in his office.

3 In the meeting room there's a table with eight chairs. There is also a projector and a screen. Gary is giving a presentation.

4 Today is Chris's first day in Force Architects. He doesn't have any furniture in his office, but he's got a computer. There are some boxes on the floor.

5 In reception there's a coffee table and a sofa. There are some chairs and magazines.

6 Ana is the company lawyer. She's got lots of bookshelves and law books in her office.

24 ● UNIT 3

2 Look again at the picture. Is there a room similar to your office or work area?

3 🎧 **3.1** Today is Chris' first day at Force Architects. Rachel, the receptionist, comes to see him. She asks Chris some questions. Tick (✓) the things that Chris has in his office. Put a cross (✗) next to the things that he doesn't have.

computer ✓	keyboard ✓	mouse ✓	printer ✗	phone ✗
pens ✓	paper ✓	diary ✗	calendar ✓	pictures on the walls ✗

4 🎧 **3.2** Chris asks Rachel some questions about the company offices. Listen and tick (✓) true or false.

		True	False
1	There isn't a canteen in the office.	☐	☐
2	There's a coffee machine upstairs.	☐	☐
3	There aren't any rooms with air conditioning.	☐	☐
4	There's a car park in the next street.	☐	☐
5	There's one parking space in the office.	☐	☐

there is/are, some/any

Read the examples and complete the grammar rules.

Positive
- There's a table with eight chairs.
- There are some boxes.

Question
- Is there a coffee machine in the office?
- Are there any parking spaces?

Negative
- There isn't a canteen in the office.
- There aren't any books.

Short answer
Yes, there is.
No, there aren't.

Write *singular* or *plural*.
- Use *there is/there's* with _____ nouns.
- Use *there are* with _____ nouns.
- Use *some* with _____ nouns in positive sentences, where we don't say the number.
- Use *any* with _____ nouns in negative sentences and questions.

📗 Pocket Book p.12

have, have got

Read the examples and the grammar rules.

Positive
- I **have** a computer and a keyboard.
- I've **got** a calendar.

Question
- Do you **have** a diary?
- Have you **got** pens and paper?

- Use both *have* and *have got* in British English.
- Use only *have* in American English.

Negative
- The computer **doesn't have** a mouse.
- We **haven't got** air conditioning in the office.

Short answer
Yes, I **do**.
No, I **haven't**.

📗 Pocket Book p.4

UNIT 3

Pronunciation

🎧 3.3 Listen and repeat the sentences.
1 There's only one printer in the office.
2 There are some chairs and magazines in reception.
3 There aren't any books in her office.
4 Are there any parking spaces?
5 I've got a calendar.
6 Has the office got air conditioning?

Practice

1 Look at the list. Tick (✓) what you have at your place of work or study.

	You	Your partner
quiet areas	☐	☐
escalators or lifts	☐	☐
a coffee machine	☐	☐
a canteen	☐	☐
a gym or fitness room	☐	☐
a car park	☐	☐
a medical centre	☐	☐
a crèche	☐	☐
a reception area	☐	☐
air conditioning	☐	☐

2 Work in pairs. Ask your partner about their place of work. Use the list in **1**.

Ask *Is there a …?* Answer *Yes, there is./No, there isn't.*
     Are there any?   *Yes, there are./No, there aren't.*

3 Work in another pair. Find out about your partner's office or work area.

Ask *Do you have a …?* Answer *Yes, I do./No, I don't.*
     Do you have any…?
or
Ask *Have you got a …?* Answer *Yes, I have./No I haven't.*

26 UNIT 3

4 Work in pairs. Look at the picture for one minute. Then close your books and write down everything in the office. Did you remember everything?

5 Work in groups. Describe your ideal place of work. Make a list of your ideas and present them to the class.

Begin   *Our ideal place of work has a/some …*
There's a …/There are some…

UNIT 3   27

Wordpower

Prepositions

1 Look at the picture of the town. You are standing outside the bank. Complete the sentences with the words in the box.

> department store   post office   seafront   tourist information office
> theatre   café   bookshop   chairs and tables

1 The _____ is on the corner of Museum Road and Seafront Road, next to the post office.
2 The _____ is between the music shop and the café.
3 The _____ is next to the tourist information office, opposite the car park.
4 The _____ is on the right of the bank.
5 The _____ is opposite the café.
6 The _____ are in front of the café.
7 The _____ is on the right of the museum.
8 The _____ is near the town centre.

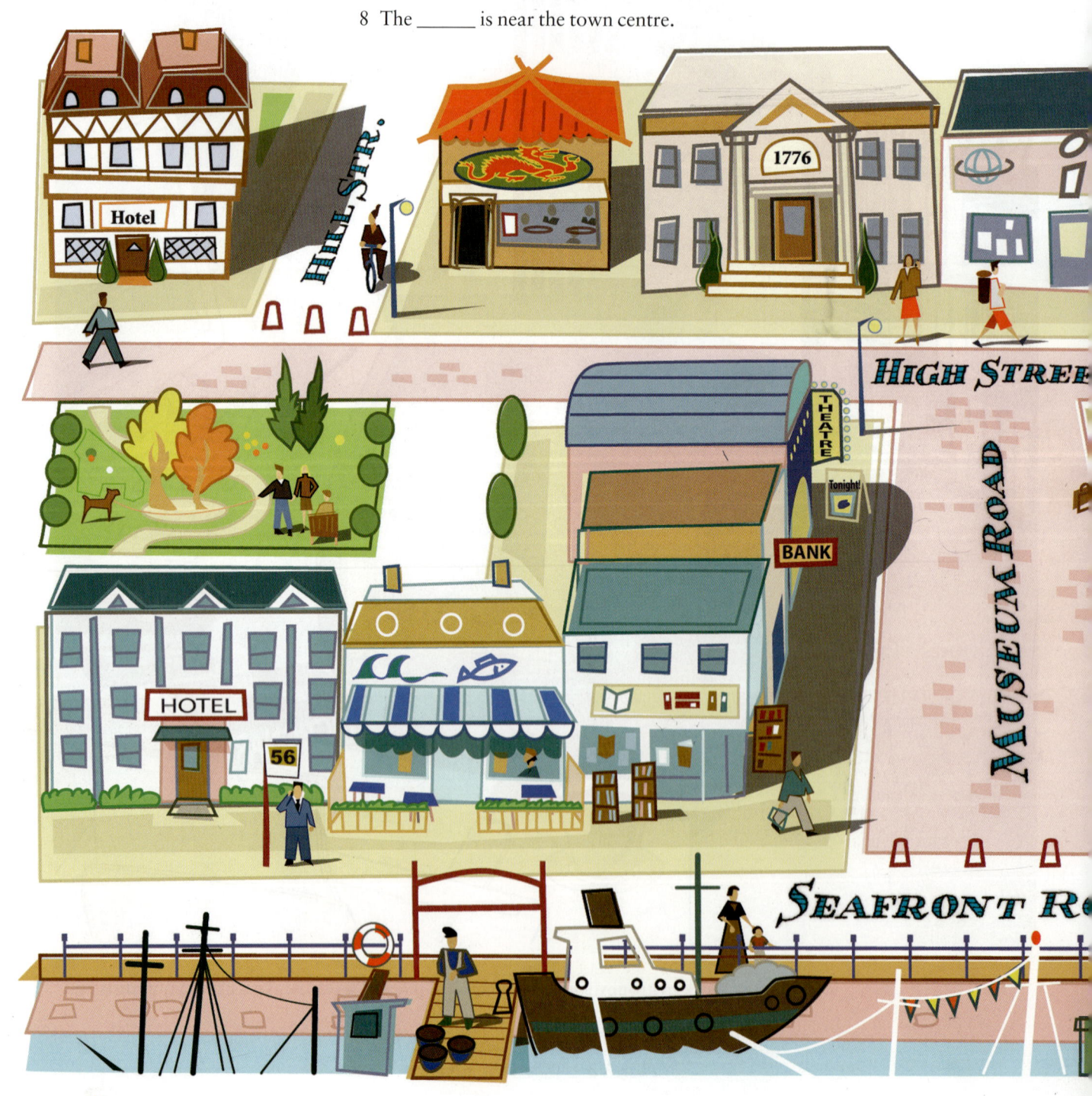

28 UNIT 3

2 🎧 **3.4** Six colleagues are on a business trip. They are trying to meet in the town centre. Mark (✗) their positions on the map.

> Katrin   Julia   Boris   Sara   Diana   Vincent

3 🎧 **3.5** Listen and write A, B, and C on the map to show where these places are.

A the Sanders Hotel
B the taxi rank
C the Italian restaurant *Il Mare*

4 🎧 **3.5** Listen again. Complete the sentences.

1 Excuse me, _____ the Sanders Hotel?

2 Excuse me, _____ taxi rank _____?

3 _____, we're _____ an Italian restaurant.

5 How do the business visitors say 'thank you'?

6 Work in pairs. Choose two places on the map. Tell your partner where you are.

UNIT 3   29

Focus on communication

Asking for and giving directions

1 Match the words and pictures a–e.

☐ bridge   ☐ pedestrian crossing
☐ square   ☐ traffic lights
☐ crossroads

2 Look at the town map. Find a–e on the map.

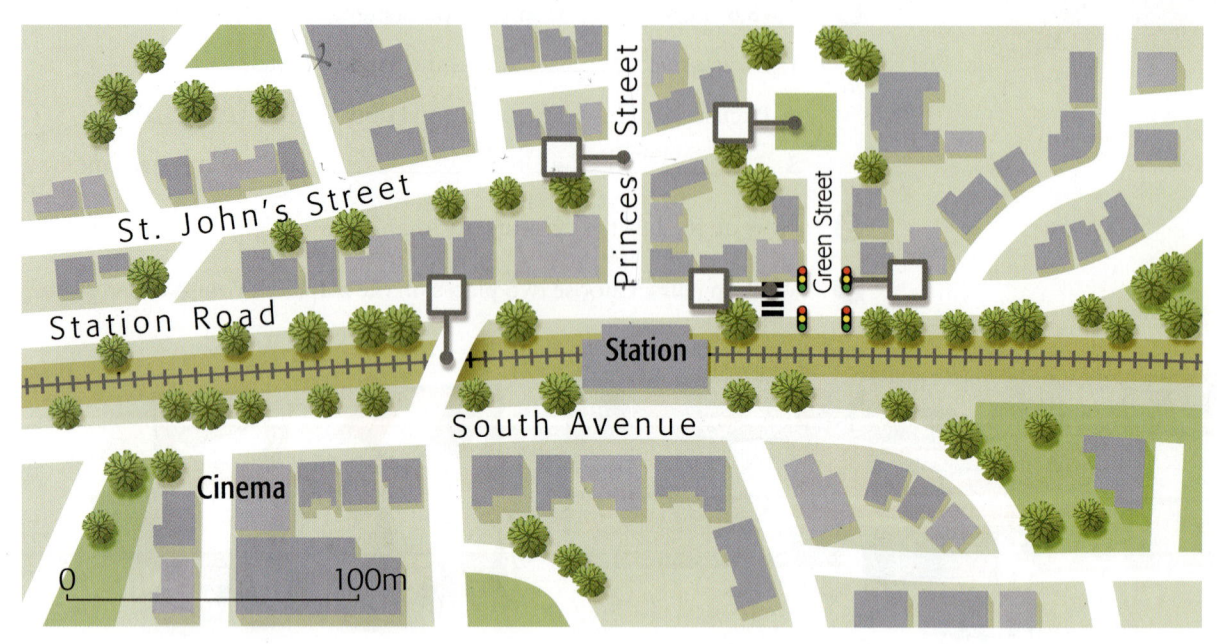

3 🎧 3.6 Listen to three conversations with visitors to the town. They are standing in front of the station on Station Road. Write the number on the map to show where these places are.

1 shopping centre   2 museum   3 sports centre

4 Work in pairs. You are on South Avenue, in front of the cinema. Ask for and give directions to four places on the map. Use phrases from the box.

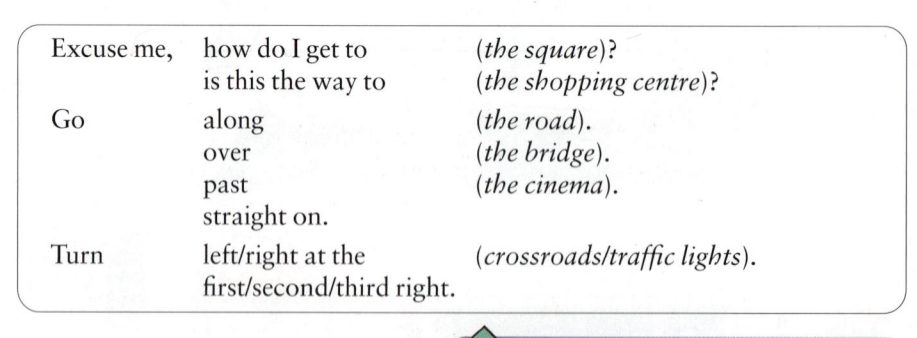

Excuse me,	how do I get to	(*the square*)?
	is this the way to	(*the shopping centre*)?
Go	along	(*the road*).
	over	(*the bridge*).
	past	(*the cinema*).
	straight on.	
Turn	left/right at the	(*crossroads/traffic lights*).
	first/second/third right.	

Pocket Book p.14

5 Write one of the conversations from **4**.

Asking for travel information

1 Look at the pictures on the left. Find the words for
1 the cost of a journey   *fare*
2 the place where you get on and off a train   _____
3 the place where you get on and off a bus   _____
4 a ticket to travel from A to B   _____
5 a ticket to travel from A to B and B to A   _____
6 something which shows you have paid   _____

30 • UNIT 3

c

d

e

2 Read the sentences. Tick (✓) to show when you use them.

Travel by	train	bus	taxi
1 How long does the journey take?	✓	✓	✓
2 What's the fare?	☐	☐	☐
3 Which platform does it leave from?	☐	☐	☐
4 Do you go to the city centre?	☐	☐	☐
5 Can you take me to the Sheraton Hotel, please?	☐	☐	☐
6 Can you tell me when to get off?	☐	☐	☐
7 Can I have a receipt, please?	☐	☐	☐
8 Keep the change.	☐	☐	☐

3 🎧 3.7 Listen to a conversation between a passenger and a ticket office clerk. Complete the chart.

Destination	
Ticket	
Fare	
Next train	at in
Platform	
Journey time	

4 🎧 3.7 Listen again and check.

5 Work in pairs. Practise the conversations.

STUDENT A

Conversation 1
You want to travel to Paris by train.
Ask Student B
- for a return to Paris
- for a receipt
- What time … ?
- Which platform … ?
- How long … ?

STUDENT B

Conversation 1
You work at a train station.
Answer Student A's questions.
- return to Paris €160
- next train: 16.30
- platform 17
- journey time: 2 hrs 50 mins

STUDENT B

Conversation 2
You want to travel to Brussels by bus.
Ask Student A
- for a single to Brussels
- for a receipt
- What time … ?
- Which bus stop … ?
- How long … ?

STUDENT A

Conversation 2
You work at a bus station.
Answer Student B's questions.
- single to Brussels €47
- next bus: 13.45
- bus stop 9
- journey time: 6 hrs 30 mins

6 Write one of the conversations you had in **5**.

UNIT 3

UNIT 4
The road to success

▼ AGENDA
▶ Past Simple
▶ Regular and irregular verbs
▶ Travel for work
▶ Leaving a message
▶ Telephone numbers
▶ Spelling

Language focus 1

1 How often do you buy a:
- guidebook?
- dictionary?
- novel?

2 Look at the information about *Lonely Planet*. Answer the questions.
1. What kind of company is *Lonely Planet*?
2. Do *Lonely Planet* only publish travel guides?
3. What can you find on their website?

Lonely Planet is the largest independent travel book company in the English-speaking world. It helps around 6 million travellers a year. They publish around 650 travel guides, maps, and phrasebooks in 15 different languages by 200 authors.

Travellers can buy digital guides from the website which has over 3 million visitors a month from about 150 different countries. They employ 400 people around the world and make over $75 million a year.

3 Read the article *The road to success*. Answer the questions.
1. What kind of travel was a new idea in 1972?
2. Why did Tony and Maureen decide to write a book about budget travel?
3. What company did Tony and Maureen start?

The road to success

In 1972 Tony and Maureen Wheeler bought a mini-van for £100 and left England on a journey to Australia. They travelled through Europe, the Middle East, and Asia. They lived very cheaply and didn't spend much money.

'Cheap, independent adventure travel was a new idea at that time', Tony says, 'and a lot of people were interested in our 11,000 mile journey. They wanted a lot of information. They asked us about the routes we followed, the places we went to, the things we saw, and where we ate. At that time there weren't any books about budget travel so we decided to write one. We didn't have a typewriter so Maureen borrowed one from work. We worked on the book in the evenings and at weekends'.

When they finished the book Tony took it to bookshops in Sydney. The buyer at one shop really liked the book and showed it to his girlfriend, who was a journalist for the *Sydney Morning Herald*. She wrote an article about it. Then a TV channel invited Tony to appear in a programme. A lot of people were interested in the book and in independent travel. More and more shops began to sell the book. It was the start of the *Lonely Planet* publishing company.

Past Simple

Read the examples and the grammar rules. Answer the question.

Positive

Regular verbs
- They **wanted** a lot of information.
- We **worked** on the book in the evenings and at weekends.

Irregular verbs
- They **bought** a mini-van for £100.
- She **wrote** an article about it.

Negative
- They **didn't spend** much money.
- We **didn't have** a typewriter.

- Use the Past Simple for finished situations and actions in the past.
- To make the Past Simple of regular verbs, add *-ed* to the end of the verb.
- To make the Past Simple of irregular verbs, see Pocket Book p.20.
- To make the negative, use *didn't* (*did not*) + infinitive (e.g. *spend, have*).

Is the Past Simple the same for all persons (*I/you/he/we*, etc.)?

Correct the mistakes.
1 He didn't worked.
2 She didn't studied.

Pocket Book p.8

Practice

1 Write the Past Simple forms of these verbs. They are all in the article *The road to success*.

Regular verbs

travel	*travelled**	follow	_____	finish	_____
live	_____	decide	_____	like	_____
want	_____	borrow	_____	show	_____
ask	_____	work	_____	invite	_____

*travelled = BrE spelling   traveled = AmE spelling

Pronunciation

🎧 **4.1** There are three ways to pronounce *-ed*. Complete the table with the verbs from **1**. Then listen and check your answers.

/d/	/t/	/ɪd/
_____	_____	_____
_____	_____	_____
_____	_____	_____
_____	_____	
_____		

2 Write the Past Simple forms of these verbs. They are all in the article *The road to success*.

Irregular verbs

| buy | _____ | go | _____ | eat | _____ | write | _____ |
| leave | _____ | see | _____ | take | _____ | begin | _____ |

Pocket Book p.20

3 Complete the information about Tony Wheeler. Use the Past Simple form of the verb in brackets.

Tony Wheeler

When Tony Wheeler _was_¹ (be) a child, he _____² (live) in Pakistan, the West Indies and the USA, so he _____³ (travel) a lot from an early age. He _____⁴ (go) to university in England and _____⁵ (study) engineering. Then he _____⁶ (get) a job with the car company Chrysler, but he only _____⁷ (work) there only for a short time. He _____⁸ (meet) his wife, Maureen, a secretary, on a park bench in Regent's Park, London in 1970 and _____⁹ (marry) her a year later.

4 Work in pairs. Correct the sentences that are not true. Use the negative form of the verb.

1 Tony worked for Chrysler for a long time.
2 He met his wife, Maureen, in Sydney.
3 They travelled to Australia by plane.
4 They decided to write a book about budget travel.
5 Maureen bought a typewriter.
6 A journalist wrote an article about the book.

Language focus 2

1 4.2 Listen to an interview with Tony Wheeler. Answer the questions.

1 Why did Tony and Maureen go to Australia?
2 Where did they write their first book?
3 How much money did they spend on their journey?

Past Simple

Read the examples and grammar rules.

Question
- **Did** you **write** your first book in Sydney?
- **Did** you **return** to London?

- Why **did** you **go** to Australia?
- How much money **did** you **take**?
- How **did** you **sell** the book?

Short answer
- Yes, we **did**.
- No, we **didn't**.

Correct the mistakes.
1 Did he returned yesterday?
2 Did they went to the USA?

Pocket Book p.8

34 UNIT 4

Practice

❶ 1 Look at the verbs in the Past Simple. What is the Present Simple form?

a arrived   _____
b lost   _____
c took   _____
d left   _____
e broke   _____
f woke up   _____

2 Work in pairs. Look at the pictures of business trips. What went wrong? Use the phrases in the box.

> take the wrong train   break his leg   wake up late   lose his luggage
> arrive late   leave his laptop in a taxi

❷ Complete the questions with a word from the box.

> Did …?   When …?   What …?   Why …?

1 _Did_ you go to work yesterday?
2 _____ did you leave school?
3 _____ did you do last weekend?
4 _____ did you begin English lessons?
5 _____ you have a holiday last year?
6 _____ you do any sport last weekend?
7 _____ did you learn in your last English lesson?
8 _____ you speak English yesterday?

❸ Work in pairs. Ask your partner the questions you made in ❷. Answer your partner's questions.

Wordpower

Travel for work

❶ Complete the word maps. Use the words from the box.

> plane   a hotel   ferry   hot   train   a factory   wet
> Hong Kong   cloudy   sunny   cold   the USA

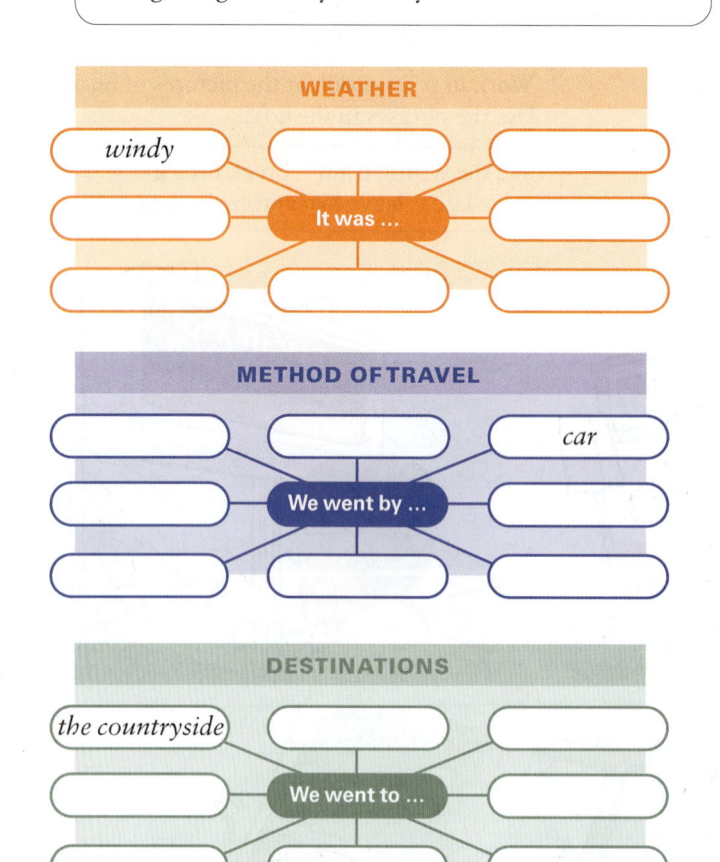

WEATHER

windy — It was … —

METHOD OF TRAVEL

— We went by … — *car*

DESTINATIONS

the countryside — We went to … —

❷ Work in pairs. What other words can you add to the word maps?

36 • UNIT 4

3 Mohammed and Laura work together. They have lunch and talk about Mohammed's last business trip. Match Laura's questions 1–8 with the answers a–h.

1 Where did you go?
2 When did you go?
3 How long did you stay there?
4 How did you travel?
5 What was the weather like?
6 Who did you go with?
7 Where did you stay?
8 Did you have a good time?

a I went last month.
b I went with our regional manager, David Wong.
c In Guangzhou we went by car and we went to Hong Kong by ferry.
d We stayed in five-star hotels all the time.
e I went to Guangzhou and Hong Kong.
f It was wet, rainy, and cold!
g Yeah, I loved it.
h Nine days.

4 🎧 4.3 Listen to Mohammed and Laura's conversation. Check your answers to **3**.

5 Work in pairs. Interview a partner about a recent work trip/holiday. Ask and answer Laura's questions in **3**.

6 Put the sentences in the correct place in the chart. Which sentence describes your business trip/holiday in **5**?

It was good.	It wasn't very good.
It was OK.	It was fabulous!
It was awful!	It was very good.

How was your trip?

Focus on communication

Leaving a message

1 Number the lines of the telephone conversation to show the right order.

☐ One moment, please. I'm sorry, the line's busy. Will you hold?
☐ Good morning. Sava Electronics.
☐ Er, no, I'll call again later. Thank you. Goodbye.
☐ Goodbye.
☐ Good morning. Can I have extension 473, please?

2 🎧 4.4 Listen and check.

3 🎧 4.4 Listen again and repeat.

4 Write the phrases from the conversation in **1** which mean:

1 I'm afraid the line's engaged. _____
2 Will you hold on? _____
3 I'll ring back later. _____

5 Work in pairs. Practise the conversation in **1**. Use the phrases from **4**.

6 Read the telephone conversation. The missing phrases are in the box below. Write the letter in the correct space.

A Good morning. Sava Electronics.
B Good morning. __d__¹ 473, please?
A Yes. One moment, please.
B Hello. _____² Carla Mann?
C No, it's her PA. I'm sorry, but she's in a meeting. _____³ ?
B Yes, please. _____⁴ ? My name's Ron Basca and the number is 01483 675 9982.
C _____⁵ ?
B Yes, 01483 675 9982.
C Thank you. _____⁶ ?
B Yes. Ron, that's R-O-N, Basca, B-A-S-C-A.
C Thank you, Mr Basca. _____⁷.
B Thanks a lot. Goodbye.

a Sorry, could you say that again?
b Can I take a message?
c Is that …?
d Can I have extension …? ✓
e Could you ask her to call me?
f I'll give her your message.
g Could you spell your name, please?

7 🎧 4.5 Listen and check your answers.

8 🎧 4.6 Listen and repeat the phrases.

9 Practise the conversation in pairs. Change roles and practise again.

Telephoning tips

1. Say telephone numbers separately. For 613875 say *six one three eight seven five*.
2. For 0 say *oh* or *zero*.
3. For 77 say *double seven*.
4. For Ext. 651 say *extension six five one*.
5. Pause after every two, three, or four numbers. For 0173-80744 say *zero one seven three … eight zero seven … double four*.

Telephone numbers

1 Work in pairs. Say the numbers.

a 0207-668350   c 022-094576
b 0269-330594   d 0044-851255

2 4.7 There is one mistake in each telephone number. Listen and correct the mistake.

a 0208-553-9075   c 75-30-6629
b 0143-4285711   d 001212-5315808

3 Work in pairs. Write three telephone numbers. Dictate them to your partner. Check your partner's answers.

Spelling

1 4.8 Listen to the recording. Write the missing letters.

d   e   j   k   n   u   x   y

(say) /eɪ/	(he) /iː/	(egg) /e/	(eye) /aɪ/	(go) /əʊ/	(bar) /ɑː/	(you) /uː/
a	b	f	i	o	r	q
h	c	l	___	___	___	___
___	___	m				w
___	___	___				
	g	s				
	p	___				
	t	*z (BrE)				
	v					
	*z (AmE)					

* AmE = zee
* BrE = zed

T = capital t
t = small t
tt = double t

2 4.8 Listen again and repeat.

3 4.9 Listen and write the nationalities.

1 *French*   2 _____   3 _____   4 _____   5 _____   6 _____

4 Work in pairs. Write the names of three countries. Spell them to your partner. Check your partner's answers.

5 Work in pairs. Practise the telephone conversation below. Use phrases from the conversation in **6** on page 38. Then change roles and practise again.

Student A
Answer the phone. Give the name of your company.

Ask the caller to hold on. Say Alex is busy with a visitor. Offer to take a message.

Ask caller to repeat phone number.

Ask caller to spell his/her name.

Reply. Say you'll give the message to Alex Jonson.

Student B

Ask to speak to Alex Jonson.

Give your message, name, and phone number.

Reply.

Spell your name.

End the conversation.

UNIT 4   39

REVIEW UNIT B

▼ AGENDA
▶ Grammar ❷, ❸, ❺
▶ Vocabulary ❶, ❹
▶ Communication ❻

This unit reviews the main language points from Units 3 and 4. Complete the exercises. Check your learning with the self-check box at the end.

❶ Vocabulary: places in a town

Write the name of the places in a town.

1 a building with art and very old objects   m _ _ _ _ _ _
2 a place where you sleep when you travel   h _ _ _ _ _
3 a place where you eat dinner   r _ _ _ _ _ _ _ _ _
4 a shop where you buy medicine   c _ _ _ _ _ _ _ _
5 a place where you watch a film   c _ _ _ _ _ _
6 a place where you get an underground train   m _ _ _ _ s _ _ _ _ _ _ _

❷ there is/are, some/any

1 Work in pairs. Think of eight things that make a town a pleasant and interesting place to live (e.g. a beautiful river, good restaurants, nightclubs, parks). Make a list.

2 Work with another partner. Find out about your partner's town. Ask questions about the things in your list.

   Ask *Is there a …?*   Answer *Yes, there is./No, there isn't.*
        Are there any …?   *Yes, there are./No, there aren't.*

3 Write three sentences about things your town has, and three sentences about things your town does not have. Use *There is/isn't a … There are some/aren't any …*

❸ have, have got

Complete the questions. Use *have* or *have got*.

Examples *Have you got* a computer?   Yes, I have.
              Do they have a boat?   No, they don't.

1 _____ any children?   Yes, I have.
2 _____ a car?   No, I haven't.
3 _____ an interesting job?   Yes, she does.
4 _____ a garden?   Yes, we do.
5 _____ a house in the country?   No, they haven't.
6 _____ a flat in the city centre?   No, he doesn't.

❹ Vocabulary: travel for work

1 Work in pairs. Write down the weather word for each picture.

a _____ b _____ c _____ d _____ e _____

2 Work in pairs. Write the travel word for each picture.

a _____ b _____ c _____ d _____

5 Past Simple

1 Complete the sentences so that they are true for you. Write the Past Simple positive or negative form of the verb.

My partner

1 I _____ a newspaper this morning. (buy)
2 I _____ dinner at home yesterday evening. (eat)
3 I _____ an email yesterday. (write)
4 I _____ shopping last Saturday morning. (go)
5 I _____ home before 8 a.m. this morning. (leave)
6 I _____ at work yesterday afternoon. (be)
7 I _____ a friend one evening last week. (meet)
8 I _____ English for more than two hours last week. (study)

2 Work in pairs. Ask your partner about the activities in ❺ 1. Tick (✓) for *Yes*, put a cross (✗) for *No*. How many of the things did you both do?

Example Student A *Did you buy a newspaper this morning?*
Student B *Yes, I did./No, I didn't.*
Student B *Did you eat dinner at home yesterday evening?*, etc.

6 Telephoning

Complete the telephone conversations. Write ONE word in each gap.

Conversation 1

A Good morning. CRT Services.
B Good morning. Can I have _____¹ 213, _____²?
A One _____³, please. I'm _____⁴, but the line's _____⁵. Will you _____⁶?
B No, I'll _____⁷ _____⁸ later. Thank you. _____⁹.
A _____¹⁰.

Conversation 2

B Hello. Is that Carla Mann?
A No, it's her secretary. I'm _____¹, but she's in a meeting. Can I _____² a _____³?
B Yes, please. _____⁴ you ask her to _____⁵ me? My _____⁶ _____⁷ Joanna Burns and my _____⁸ is 020 8755 8331.
A Sorry, _____⁹ you _____¹⁰ that again?
B Yes, 020 8755 8331.
C Thank you. Could you _____¹¹ your _____¹², please?
B Yes. Joanna, that's J-O-A-N-N-A, Burns, that's B-U-R-N-S.
C Thank you, Ms Burns. I'll _____¹³ her your _____¹⁴.
B Thanks a lot. Goodbye.

Look at the self-check box. Tick the areas you need to review again.

SELF-CHECK BOX	Yes	No	Pocket Book
• Vocabulary: places in a town			
• *there is/are, some/any*			12
• *have, have got*			4
• Vocabulary: travel for work			
• Past Simple			8
• Telephoning			17

REVIEW UNIT B 41

UNIT 5
The world's largest industry

▼ AGENDA
- ▶ Mass and count nouns
- ▶ *some, a lot of/much/many*
- ▶ Food file
- ▶ Offers and requests
- ▶ Eating and drinking

Language focus 1

1
1 Do many tourists visit your country?
2 Which places do they visit?
3 Which countries do they come from?

2 The words in A are in the article *The world's no. 1 industry*. Match them with their meaning in B.

A		B	
1	employment	a	one million million, 1000 000 000 000
2	trillion	b	a place to stay, for example, a hotel
3	export	c	TV, newspapers, magazines, etc.
4	transportation	d	work, a job
5	package holidays	e	holidays which include travel, accommodation, and food
6	media	f	to sell and send goods to another country
7	accommodation	g	the way we travel, e.g. planes, cars, trains, boats, etc.

3 Read the article *The world's no. 1 industry*. Answer the questions.
1 How many people work in the tourist industry?
2 Why did tourism grow?
3 What can people book using the Internet?

The world's no. 1 industry

Tourism is the largest industry in the world. It gives employment to millions of people and is important for a country's economy. It employs 200 million people: 8% of jobs around the world. It makes $3.6 trillion every year and is the number one export in 60 countries.

Tourism grew because of better transportation – rail travel in the 1840s, sea travel in the 1900s, and air travel in the 1950s. The introduction of package holidays in the 1960s offered people an easy, inexpensive way to travel abroad. Another reason was the development of the media. From the 1900s travel companies used newspapers to advertise their products. In the 1960s television showed holiday programmes and gave people travel advice. Tourists can now get travel information and book their flights and accommodation on the Internet.

42 UNIT 5

4 How do we say these decades?

1 1900s 2 1950s 3 1960s 4 1990s

Which decade were you born in? *I was born in …*

5 Work in pairs. Put *do*, *does*, or *did* in the sentences to make questions about *The world's no. 1 industry*. Ask and answer the questions.

1 How much money tourism make?
2 When rail travel get better?
3 How travel companies use newspapers?
4 What information people get from the Internet?

Mass and count nouns

Count nouns
Count nouns have a singular and plural form.
newspaper – newspapers
company – companies
industry – industries
We can use *a*, *an*, and *the* with them.
a newspaper, an industry, the company

Mass nouns
Mass nouns do not have a plural form.
We do not use *a* or *an* with them.
transportation, travel, information

📖 Pocket Book p.5

Practice

1 Read these sentences and decide if the word in *italics* is a count or mass noun.

1 In many *countries* the economy needs *tourism*.
2 We had a great *holiday* but we lost our *luggage*.
3 The *weather* in Germany in the summer is great – lots of *sunshine* and no *rain*.
4 The travel *company* offers *work* to local *people*.
5 The increase in *travel* means more *traffic* – more *planes* and more *cars*.

2 Which words in the plural are possible?

1 Have you got the *luggage/luggages*?
2 I bought some *newspaper/newspapers*.
3 The *accommodation/accommodations* in Sydney *is/are* very good.
4 The *tourist/tourists is/are* visiting our village.
5 His *advice/advices was/were* very useful.
6 *Tourism/Tourisms helps/help employment/employments*.

UNIT 5 43

Language focus 2

1 How do we say these years?
1 1950   2 1980   3 1993   4 2001   5 2012

2 How do we say these numbers?
1 166   2 305   3 559   4 732   5 2.3

3 🎧 5.1 Listen to an interview with a journalist and an official from the World Tourism Organization. Complete the Tourist Arrivals chart with the years.

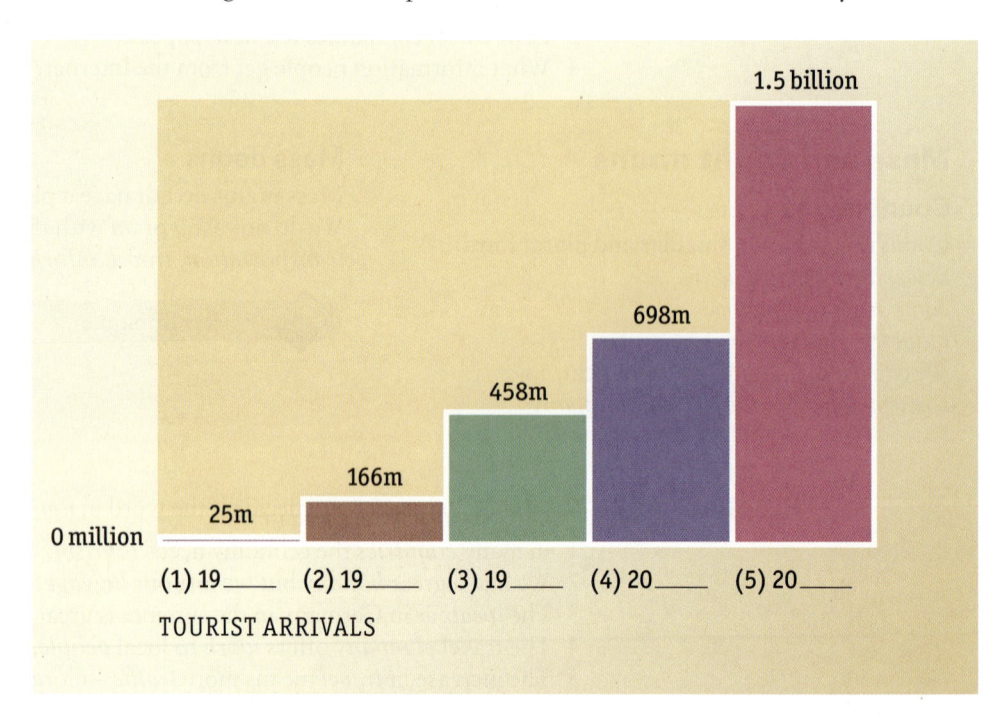

1.5 billion
698m
458m
166m
25m
0 million

(1) 19____ (2) 19____ (3) 19____ (4) 20____ (5) 20____

TOURIST ARRIVALS

4 Match the pictures with the place.
1 jungle   2 coast   3 a lodge   4 a hotel resort

5 Costa Rica is a popular country with ecotourists. What are ecotourists?

  a people who want to have a cheap holiday
  b people who want to make money from tourism
  c people who want to have a holiday and care about the environment

6 🎧 5.2 Listen to a journalist and a tourism expert talking about ecotourism. Fill in the blanks.

  1 A visitor to Costa Rica spends $____ on average.
  2 A visitor to France spends $____ on average.
  3 The income for local people from ecotourism is about $____.
  4 The total income for Costa Rica last year was $____ billion.

---

some, a lot of/much/many

Read the examples and complete the grammar rules.

Positive
- Can you give me **some** figures?
- I'd like **some** information about that.
- There are **a lot of** popular countries.
- $1,000 dollars is **a lot of** money in Costa Rica.

Negative
- There weren't **many** international tourists then.
- There isn't **much** demand for big hotel resorts.

Questions
- How **many** tourists were there in 1950?
- How **much** money does an average visitor spend?
- Does ecotourism make **much** money for Costa Ricans?

Write *positive*, *negative*, or *questions*.
- Use *some* and *a lot of* with both mass and count nouns in _____ sentences.
- Use *many* with count nouns in _____ sentences and in questions.
- Use *much* with mass nouns in _____ sentences and in _____.

📘 Pocket Book p.5

Practice

1 Work in pairs. Ask for and give information about the chart on p.44 using *How many …?*

  Example Ask *How many tourists were there in 1950?*
  Answer *Twenty five million.*

2 Work in pairs. Ask for and give information about the information in **6** using *How much …?*

  Example Ask *How much does a tourist spend in Costa Rica?*
  Answer *$1,000 on average.*

3 Work in pairs. Write questions to ask another student about a recent holiday. Use *How much …?* or *How many …?*

  1 people/go with?   *How many people did you go with?*
  2 money/spend?   _____
  3 days/stay?   _____
  4 places/visit?   _____
  5 luggage/take?   _____
  6 problems/have?   _____
  7 food/eat?   _____
  8 wild animals/see?   _____

UNIT 5 45

Wordpower

Food file

1 Match the words with the food in pictures a–v.

[a] apples	[ ] cheese	[ ] mineral water	[ ] strawberries
[ ] bananas	[ ] chicken	[ ] mushrooms	[ ] tomatoes
[ ] beef	[ ] chocolate cake	[ ] onions	[ ] tea
[ ] beer	[ ] fish	[ ] oranges	[ ] yogurt
[ ] broccoli	[ ] ice cream	[ ] orange juice	
[ ] carrots	[ ] milk	[ ] potatoes	

Fruit

Meat and fish

Drinks

Dairy products

Desserts

Vegetables

Pronunciation

🎧 5.3 Look at the different stress patterns. Listen and repeat the words.

A	B	C
●.	●..	.●.
apples	broccoli	bananas
carrots	oranges	potatoes
chicken	strawberries	tomatoes
chocolate		
mushrooms		
onions		
yogurt		

2 Work in pairs. Look at the pictures in **1**. Test your partner.

Example Student A *What's picture q?*
Student B *Potatoes.*

Using a dictionary

1 Read the dictionary extracts. How does the dictionary show:
  a a count or countable noun?
  b a mass or uncountable noun?

banana /bəˈnɑːnə/ noun [C] a curved fruit with yellow skin that grows in hot countries: *a bunch of bananas.*

tea /tiː/ noun 1 [U] the dried leaves (called tea leaves) of the tea bush 2 [U] a hot drink made by pouring boiling water onto tea leaves 3 [C] a cup of tea: *Two teas, please.*

2 Work in pairs. Which words in *Food file* are count nouns? Which are mass or uncountable nouns? Write C (count) or M (mass) next to the word.

3 Look at the definitions of these words. Which words can we use with *advice*, *information*, and *luggage* to make them countable?

	Mass/Uncountable	Countable
a	advice	_____
b	information	_____
c	luggage	_____

advice /ədˈvaɪs/ **noun** [U] an opinion that you give sb about what they should do: *Let me give you some **advice**.*

▶ Advice is uncountable. We say *a piece of advice* (not 'an advice') *and a lot of advice* (not 'advices').

information /ˌɪnfəˈmeɪʃn/ noun [U] **information (on/about sb/sth)** knowledge or facts: *For further information please send for our fact sheet.* • *Can you give me some more information about evening classes in Italian, please?*

▶ The word information is uncountable. When we are talking about a single item, we say *a bit / piece of information* (not 'an information').

luggage /ˈlʌɡɪdʒ/ noun [U] bags, suitcases, etc. used for carrying sb's clothes and things on a journey: *'How much luggage are you taking with you?' 'Only one suitcase.'* • *You're only allowed one piece of **hand luggage*** (= a bag that you carry with you on the plane).

Definitions taken from the Oxford Wordpower Dictionary © Oxford University Press 2006.

4 Work in pairs. Ask and answer these questions.

Where can you find tourist information in your country?
Can you give me advice about travelling in your country?
How much luggage do you usually take on holiday?

UNIT 5 47

Focus on communication

Offers and requests, eating and drinking

1 🎧 **5.4** Jon Dunn visits Pete May of Novac. Listen to the conversation and answer the questions.

1 Is this their first meeting?
2 What does Jon ask Elena to bring?

2 Read the extract from the conversation. The missing parts are in the box below. Write the letter in the space.

J Hi, Pete. Good to see you again. How's everything?
P Oh, fine, thanks. What about you?
J Very busy right now. A lot of travelling.
P Yes, I can see that. __b__¹ take your coat?
J Thanks.
P ____² something to drink? A coffee, a cold drink?
J Yeah, ____³ a coffee, please.
P (on intercom) Oh, Elena, er ____⁴ bring us two coffees, please? Thanks … Well, Jon, we've got a lot to do today. ____⁵ begin with the programme?
J Yes, OK. Oh, ____⁶ give me a couple of minutes? I need to make a call.
P Of course. Go ahead.

a Shall I …?	d Would you like …?
b Can I …? ✓	e Can you … ?
c Could you …?	f I'd like …

3 🎧 **5.4** Listen again. Check your answers.

Pronunciation

1 🎧 **5.5** Listen to the questions from the conversation. The underlined words are stressed.

1 Can I <u>take</u> your coat?
2 Would you <u>like</u> something to <u>drink</u>?
3 Can you <u>bring</u> us two <u>coffees</u>, please?
4 Shall I <u>begin</u> with the <u>programme</u>?
5 Could you <u>give</u> me a couple of <u>minutes</u>?

2 🎧 **5.5** Listen to the questions again and repeat.

---

4 Work in pairs. Practise the conversation in **2**.

5 🎧 **5.6** Later, Jon and Pete have lunch. Listen to their conversation. Tick (✓) what they order on the menu.

THE RIVERSIDE BISTRO

TODAY'S SPECIALS

Starters

Tomato and carrot soup	£3.40
Salmon pâté with toast	£4.95
Grilled aubergines	£3.95

Main course

Chicken casserole	£9.50
Beef in red wine	£11.50
Mushroom quiche	£6.75
Onion and potato omlette	£6.75

All dishes served with vegetables or a side salad

Desserts

Selection of cheeses	£4.50
Ice cream	£2.95
Chocolate mousse	£3.90
Fresh fruit salad	£3.90

Drinks

Red/white house wine (bottle)	£9.99
(glass)	£2.95
Beer	£2.50
Mineral water (still or sparkling)	£2.10
Fruit juices	£2.15
Tea	£1.60
Coffee	£1.75

6 🎧 **5.6** Listen to their conversation again. Tick (✓) the phrases you hear.

Offers	Requests	Ordering
What would you like …? ☐	Could I …? ☐	I'll have … ☐
Would you like …? ☐	Can I …? ☐	I'd like … ☐
Shall I …? ☐	Can you …? ☐	
	Could you …? ☐	

📘 Pocket Book p.16

7 Work in groups of three. Order a meal at the Riverside Bistro. Use the menu in **5** and the phrases in the box in **6**.

Waiter/Waitress
1 … ready …?
5 So, that's … vegetables, or …?
8 Right. … to drink?
11 Thank you.

Host
2 What/like …?
4 And I …
7 And I …
10 I …

Guest
3 I'll …
6 I …
9 Yes, I …

8 Change roles and practise again.

9 Write your conversation.

UNIT 5 49

UNIT 6
The best way to travel

▼ AGENDA
- Comparative and superlative adjectives
- Dates
- Money
- Welcoming a visitor

Language focus

1 Work in pairs. When you travel, do you prefer to go by:
- car?
- plane?
- train?
- boat?

2 Martina Cooke is a travel writer. Read her article about travelling across Australia. Which sentences are true or false?

		true	false
1	The plane from Sydney to Perth is more expensive than the train.	☐	☐
2	There are fewer trains than flights between Sydney and Perth.	☐	☐
3	Trains are more harmful to the environment than planes.	☐	☐
4	Travelling by train across Australia is more boring than flying.	☐	☐
5	Martina thinks taking the train is better than flying.	☐	☐

By plane or by train?

There are two main ways to travel from Sydney to Perth: by plane or by train. It's a 2,700 mile journey, so flying is much easier than going by train.

Flying with the Australian airline Qantas takes four hours. The Indian Pacific train takes three nights. So flying is much quicker! A one-way plane ticket Sydney-Perth is $275 but the train is $680. So flying is also a lot cheaper. The flights are also more frequent than the train: there are flights every day but there are only two trains a week. So, why get the train?

Although the Indian Pacific is slower than the plane, the train is much better for the environment. It is also a more exciting journey across Australia. You can see the Blue Mountains, the Outback, and the Nullarbor Plain. And obviously the train is bigger so you can walk around, go to the restaurant car, and meet more people. It's a wonderful experience. I went on the train in 2006, and I can't remember a journey when I was happier.

Comparative adjectives

Complete the table with comparative adjectives from page 50.

	Adjective	Comparative
Regular One syllable	quick	_quicker_
	cheap	_____
	slow	_____
	few	_____
	big	_____
Two syllables ending in -y	easy	_easier_
	happy	_____
Two or more syllables	exciting	_more exciting_
	frequent	_____
	expensive	_____
	harmful	_____
	boring	_____
Irregular	good	better
	bad	worse

Read the grammar rules and answer the question.

One-syllable adjectives
- Add *-er* to the end of the adjective.

Two-syllable adjectives ending in -y
- Change the *-y* to *-i* and add *-er* to the end of the adjective.

Other adjectives with two or more syllables
- Put *more* before the adjective.

We put *much* or *a lot* before a comparative to show a bigger difference.

What happens to one-syllable adjectives with one short vowel and ending in one consonant, e.g. *big*, *wet*?

Pocket Book p.2

Practice

1 6.1 After her journey on the Indian Pacific Railway, Martina Cooke went on an excursion to the Blue Mountains. Listen and answer the questions.

1. Were there many people in the Blue Mountains?
2. Was Martina on her own?
3. Look at the pictures. Which activity did Martina do?

a b c

2 Work in pairs. Write the comparative form of the adjectives. Use the information in the grammar box to help you.

1. busy — _busier_
2. crowded — _____
3. clean — _____
4. expensive — _____
5. quiet — _____
6. old — _____
7. young — _____
8. adventurous — _____

3 6.1 Listen to the interview again. Martina uses the comparative form of the adjectives in **2**. Check your answers.

4 Complete the sentence with a comparative adjective. Give your opinion.

Example *Learning computer science is more difficult than learning history.*

1. Living in the country is _____ than living in the city centre.
2. Eating at home is _____ than going to restaurants.
3. Skiing holidays are _____ than beach holidays.
4. Reading a novel is _____ than reading the newspaper.
5. Motorbikes are _____ than cars.

UNIT 6   51

Language focus 2

1 Read the article *The Best in the World*. Which opinions do you agree with? Which do you disagree with?

The Best in the World

Condé Naste Traveller asked its readers to choose their favourite travel destinations. Here are the results of the survey.

■ Countries
Italy was the most popular tourist destination and readers also think it is the country with the best food. The magazine's readers think New Zealand is the country with the nicest climate, although South Africa is the country with the most attractive scenery. India is the country with the most fascinating culture while Australia has the friendliest people.

■ Cities
The most interesting city for culture was Barcelona. Rome came first for architecture and was the prettiest city in the survey. The cleanest city was Singapore. Finally, the readers chose Venice as the safest city in the world and Melbourne was the most user-friendly, the easiest city to explore.

Superlative adjectives

Complete the table with superlative adjectives from the article *The Best in the World*. What are the comparative adjectives?

	Adjective	Comparative	Superlative
Regular			
One syllable	clean	_____	the _____ cleanest
	nice	_____	the _____
	safe	_____	the _____
Two syllables ending in -y	friendly	_____	the _____ friendliest
	pretty	_____	the _____
	easy	_____	the _____
Two or more syllables	popular	more _____	the most _____ popular
	attractive	_____	the most _____
	fascinating	_____	the most _____
	interesting	_____	the most _____
Irregular			
	good	_____	the _____
	bad	_____ worse	the _____ worst

One-syllable adjectives
- Add -est to the end of the adjective.

Two-syllable adjectives ending in -y
- Change the -y to -i and add _____ to the end of the adjective.

Other adjectives with two or more syllables
- Put _____ before the adjective.

📕 Pocket Book p.2

Practice

1 🎧 **6.2** Listen to an interview with a travel consultant. She is giving the cost of a short stay in some big cities. Complete the table.

Cost of a short stay in a major city

	US $
Average cost	____
London	900
Tokyo	860
New York	670
Paris	____
Milan	570
Seoul	560
Madrid	____
Lisbon	540
Moscow	490
Warsaw	490
Budapest	410
Sydney	400
Bangkok	____
São Paulo	____
Prague	____

2 Complete the sentences with the comparative or superlative form of the adjective in brackets.

1 The _____ cost for a short stay is in London. (high)
2 A short stay in Moscow is _____ than in Tokyo. (cheap)
3 The cost of a short stay in Seoul is _____ than in Sydney. (high)
4 You pay _____ prices in Milan than in New York. (low)
5 A short stay in Warsaw is _____ than in Budapest. (expensive)
6 The _____ cost is in Prague. (low)

3 Work in groups. Think of cities you know. Which is the best city for a short stay? Which is the worst? Compare the two cities. Use the adjectives in the box and your own ideas. Use the comparative or superlative form.

| beautiful | ugly | cheap | expensive | fun | boring |
| old | modern | large | small | dangerous | enjoyable |

Example *I think Madrid is better than London because Madrid is more fun and less expensive.*

UNIT 6 • 53

Wordpower

Dates

❶ Work in pairs. What are the two ways of saying these dates?

1 1st May
2 2nd April
3 10th March
4 19th August
5 24th September

❷ 🎧 6.3 Listen and check your answers.

❸ 🎧 6.4 Listen and underline the number you hear.

1 7th/17th
2 13th/30th
3 6th/16th
4 12th/20th

Pronunciation

/ð/   /θ/

the four**th** of June

🎧 6.5 Listen and repeat the dates.

1 3rd April – the third of April
2 4th June – the fourth of June
3 20th March – the twentieth of March
4 23rd September – the twenty-third of September
5 13th November – the thirteenth of November
6 30th December – the thirtieth of December

---

❹ Look at the British English and the American English ways of writing and saying dates. What is the difference?

BrE
8/9/07
the eighth of September two thousand and seven

AmE
8/9/07
August ninth two thousand and seven

❺ Work in pairs. Say these dates first in the British English way and then in the American English way.

1 1/2/99
2 6/8/00
3 11/6/06
4 7/5/07
5 3/4/01
6 2/10/10

❻ 🎧 6.6 Listen and check your answers.

Money

❶ Match the words in **A** with their meaning in **B**.

A	B
1 coins	a a card you use to buy things on credit
2 a note (AmE = a bill)	b real money that you carry with you
3 a credit card	c a place often outside a bank where you get money using your bank card
4 a debit card	d metal money
5 a cash machine (AmE = ATM)	e a card you use to pay directly from your bank account
6 cash	f paper money

2 🎧 **6.7** Listen to three conversations where people have problems paying. Match pictures a–c below with the conversations in ❸.

3 Complete the sentences from the conversations with the words from ❶.

1 Passenger 1   That's the problem. You have a fifty-euro _____.
                       The machine doesn't accept big _____.
    Passenger 2   Oh no!
    Passenger 1   Do you have any _____?

2 Waiter   We don't accept any cards.
    Customer   Oh no!
    Waiter   Do you have _____?
    Customer   No.
    Waiter   I'm very sorry sir, but we have to go together to a _____, to get the money.

3 Call centre operator   The cost is €220.
    Customer   Can I pay by _____ card?
    Call centre operator   Yes. It's more expensive to pay by _____ card. It's … an extra €5.
    Customer   Ah. Uhm, I also have my _____ card. Maestro.

4 🎧 **6.7** Listen again and check your answers to ❸.

5 Choose the right word.
1 Are you happy with the money you *earn/win* in your job?
2 What do you like to spend your money *on/at/to*? Clothes? Food? Going out?
3 Do you prefer to pay for things *in/by* cash or *in/by* debit card?
4 What do you do with your *receipts/recipes* after shopping? Throw them away? Keep them?
5 What was the last time you bought something expensive *by/with* your credit card?

6 Work in groups. Discuss the sentences in ❺.

UNIT 6   55

Focus on communication

Welcoming a visitor

1 Work in pairs. Imagine you are welcoming a foreign visitor to your place of work for the first time. Think of five questions you can ask the visitor.

2 🎧 **6.8, 6.9** Listen to two conversations in which people welcome visitors. Tick (✓) the topics they talk about.

	Conversation 1	Conversation 2
• the visitor's journey	☐	☐
• the visit	☐	☐
• home town/country	☐	☐
• work	☐	☐
• travel and holidays	☐	☐
• accommodation	☐	☐

3 🎧 **6.8** Listen to the first conversation again. Tick (✓) the questions you hear.

the visitor's journey

How was your journey? ☐
_____

home town/country

Do you come from … (Dublin)? ☐
Do you live in … (Barcelona)? ☐
Where were you born? ☐

the visit

Are you here on business or on holiday? ☐
Is this your first visit to … (Dublin)? ☐
_____
_____

travel and holidays

Do you travel a lot for work? ☐
Where do you spend your holidays? (BrE) ☐
Where do you go on vacation? (AmE) ☐
_____
_____

work

What do you do? ☐
Who do you work for? ☐
Where do you work? ☐

accommodation

What's your hotel like? ☐
_____

Pocket Book p.18

4 🎧 **6.9** Listen to the second conversation again. Write the questions.

MR ABBOTT   Welcome to New York, Ms Peto. _____¹?
MS PETO   Yes, it was fine, thanks. It's great to be here.
MR ABBOTT   _____² in New York?
MS PETO   Yes, it is. It's a very exciting city.
MR ABBOTT   It sure is. _____³?
MS PETO   Only four days. I leave on Friday.
MR ABBOTT   Oh, that's too bad. _____⁴?
MS PETO   Yes, quite a lot. I was in London last week and next week I go to Germany.
MR ABBOTT   _____⁵?
MS PETO   Yes, I find it interesting. But on a business trip there isn't any time to see the places you want to see.
MR ABBOTT   No, that's true. _____⁶?
MS PETO   Oh yes, the hotel's great, thanks.
MR ABBOTT   Good. Now, let me introduce you to some of my colleagues …

5 Add the questions from **4** to the correct group in **3**.

6 Work in pairs. Practise welcoming a visitor. Choose questions from the table in **3**.

Host	Visitor
Welcome visitor and introduce yourself.	
	Greet host.
Ask about journey.	
	Reply.
Ask if first visit.	
	Reply and give more information.
Ask how long/here for.	
	Say only two days.
Ask where visitor lives and works.	
	Reply. Ask host same question.
Ask about travel for work.	
	Reply and give more information. Ask host same question.
Begin introductions with colleagues.	

7 Change roles and practise the conversation in **6** again.

UNIT 6   57

REVIEW UNIT C

▼ AGENDA
▶ Grammar ❶ – ❸
▶ Vocabulary ❹, ❺
▶ Communication ❻, ❼

❶ Mass and count nouns

Work in pairs. Are these words mass or count nouns? Write M (mass) or C (count).

newspaper	___	traffic	___	tomato	___
transportation	___	banana	___	work	___
travel	___	money	___	apple	___
company	___	industry	___	luggage	___
information	___	plane	___	tourist	___
potato	___	wine	___		

❷ a lot of, much, many

Complete the sentences with *a lot of*, *much*, or *many*.

1 How _____ people are in your company?
2 I visit _____ companies every day.
3 It doesn't cost _____ money to go on the train.
4 I get _____ emails in the morning.
5 How _____ luggage do people take on holiday?
6 We don't have _____ visitors at our office.
7 I don't need _____ time for lunch, just thirty minutes.

❸ Comparative and superlative adjectives

Write the comparative and superlative forms of these adjectives.

		Comparative	Superlative			Comparative	Superlative
1	few	_____	_____	7	big	_____	_____
2	quick	_____	_____	8	good	_____	_____
3	easy	_____	_____	9	bad	_____	_____
4	dangerous	_____	_____	10	friendly	_____	_____
5	crowded	_____	_____	11	expensive	_____	_____
6	happy	_____	_____	12	clean	_____	_____

❹ Vocabulary: dates

What are these dates in British English and in American English?
1 9/1/99   2 12/3/00   3 11/4/02   4 7/8/90   5 2/10/72

❺ Vocabulary: money

1 Work in pairs. Write down the money word for each picture.

a   b   c   d

58 ● REVIEW UNIT C

2 Correct the mistake in each sentence.
   a I spent $200 with food when I was at the conference.
   b Most workers in this country win more than $1,000 a month.
   c After you get a taxi, always get a recipe from the driver.
   d I don't have my credit card so I have to pay through cash.
   e I paid for my flight in credit card.

6 Offers and requests

Work in pairs. Make offers and requests and reply to them.

Student A

1 Offer to take a visitor's coat.
2 Offer a visitor something to drink.
3 Ask a colleague to help you with a problem.
4 Ask a friend to post a letter for you.

Student B

1 Offer to take a visitor to his/her hotel.
2 Offer to carry a visitor's suitcase.
3 Ask a friend to drive you to the station.
4 Ask a waiter to bring you two coffees.

7 Welcoming a visitor

1 Work in pairs. Write five questions you can ask a visitor from another country. Ask about the visitor's:

- journey
- visit to your country
- home town/country
- work
- travel/holidays

2 Work with another partner. Ask the questions you wrote in 7 1. Ask and answer your partner's questions.

Look at the self-check box. Tick the areas you need to review again.

SELF-CHECK BOX	Yes	No	Pocket Book
• Mass and count nouns			5
• *a lot of*, *much*, *many*			5
• Comparative and superlative adjectives			2
• Vocabulary: dates			25
• Vocabulary: money			
• Offers and requests			16
• Welcoming a visitor			18

REVIEW UNIT C

UNIT 7
Life in the fast lane

▼ AGENDA
▶ Present Continuous
▶ Present trends
▶ Word partners
▶ Making and changing arrangements 🎧

Language focus 1

① Match the words in the box with their meaning.

| a a politician | b freelance | c an election | d politics |

1 the time when people choose a new leader, government, etc. by voting   _____
2 the work of the government   _____
3 a person who is in or wants to be in the government   _____
4 working for different organizations, not one employer   _____

② 🎧 **7.1** Listen to the first part of an interview with Kazuko Negoro, a freelance journalist. Answer the questions.
1 What does Kazuko write about?
2 Who does she write for?

③ 🎧 **7.2** Listen to the second part of the interview. Answer the questions.
1 What is Kazuko writing about this week?
2 What special report is she preparing?

Present Continuous

Read the examples and the grammar rules.

Positive
- I'm writing about the elections.
- I'm interviewing politicians.

Negative
- This week I'm not making any trips by car.

| Question | Short answer |
- Are you **travelling** a lot? — Yes, I am.
- Are you **interviewing** people for that project? — No, I'm not.

- Use the Present Continuous to talk about current activities.
- To make the Present Continuous use *am/is/are* + *-ing* form of the verb.

📘 Pocket Book p.9

60 ● UNIT 7

Practice

1 Read the sentences about Kazuko Negoro. Write R next to regular activities and C next to current activities.

1 Kazuko usually works from home. _____
2 This week she's making a lot of plane trips. _____
3 She travels a lot. _____
4 At present she's working on a project for a TV company. _____
5 She's interviewing a politician at the moment. _____
6 She often goes to Japan. _____

2 Match the verbs in **1** to the tense: Present Simple or Present Continuous.

3 Match the questions in **A** to the answers in **B**.

A
1 Where do you work?
2 Where are you working?
3 Where do you stay?
4 Where are you staying?

B
a At the same hotel every year.
b In London for two days, then in Rome for two more.
c In an office in New York.
d In our Mexico office. Just for one month.

4 Which of the questions in **3** are about a regular activity? Which are about a current activity?

Pronunciation

We often use contractions in the Present Continuous.
'm = am   's = is   're = are

1 🎧 7.3 Listen and repeat the examples.

1 He's working here.
2 You're winning the game.
3 We're going on holiday.
4 I'm listening to the radio.
5 She's helping them.
6 They're playing football.

2 Make the sentences in **1** negative.

Example *He isn't working here.*

3 🎧 7.4 Listen and repeat the negative sentences.

I'm doing a six-month computer course.

I'm studying for university exams.

I'm preparing for an important business trip to the US.

I'm travelling round the world before I start my first job.

5 Work in groups. Talk about your current work and leisure activities. Ask questions to get more information.

UNIT 7   61

Language focus 2

1 The words in **A** are in the article *Holiday? I'm too busy*. Match them with their meaning in **B**.

A
1 to damage
2 to take time off
3 survey
4 to encourage
5 sick leave

B
a to suggest something is a good idea
b a way to find a lot of people's opinion about a topic
c to make something worse
d time when you cannot go to work because you are ill
e not to go to work

2 Work in pairs. Discuss the questions.

1 How many days holiday do you have in your work/studies?
2 What did you do on your last day off from work/studying?
3 When did you last go away?
4 If you go on holiday, do you feel guilty because you are not working?

3 Read the article *Holiday? I'm too busy* and answer the questions.

1 How many US workers are not going on holiday this year?
2 Why are people not going on holiday?
3 Are companies happy because their employees don't go on holiday?

Holiday? I'm too busy

A recent survey shows that US workers are taking fewer holidays this year and are working harder than before. In fact 40% of US workers are not going on holiday at all this summer.

Present trends

Complete the examples of present trends from the article. Answer the question.

- US workers _____ fewer holidays this year.
- People _____ also _____ shorter holidays than before.
- In the USA the situation _____ serious.
- Workers _____ their health.

What tense do we use to talk about a present trend?
Find other examples of present trends in the article.

📗 Pocket Book p.9

Practice

1 Complete the sentences so they describe present trends in your country. Use verbs from the box in the Present Continuous.

go up ↑	go down ↓	not change →
increase	decrease	stay the same
rise	fall	

1 The cost of living _isn't changing_.
2 The number of people without a job _____.
3 Sales of mobile phones _____.
4 The prices of houses and flats _____.
5 The birth rate _____.
6 The number of people who smoke _____.

2 Talk about the trends in **1**. What are the reasons? Give examples of other present trends in your country.

People are also having shorter holidays than before. Most employees now only go away for seven days at a time. For many people in the US a two-week holiday is a dream.

So why are workers not going on holiday? There are many reasons. In one British survey a third of workers said they were too busy to take a holiday, while one in five said that they forgot.

In the USA the situation is becoming serious and companies are encouraging their employees to leave the office more. At PriceWaterhouseCoopers the company sends email messages to workers who don't take holiday. The messages tell them to use their holiday time.

These companies know that workers are damaging their health because they do not take holidays. And in the end, many of these overworked employees have to take time off – as sick leave. ■

UNIT 7

Wordpower

Word partners

❶ Look at the picture. What is the man's problem?

❷ Read the interview with Marie Noiret. Answer the questions.
1 How many hours does Marie work a day?
2 What time does she get to work?
3 What does she do in the afternoon?
4 What change did they make in the office?
5 Does she go home by train?
6 What sport does she do?

Europa Magazine

Surviving stress

Marie Noiret
Managing Director, Toulouse

I work twelve hours a day. I get to work at 7 a.m. and I do two hours' work before everyone else arrives at the office. I generally make phone calls and appointments to visit customers. I get emails all day and try to reply immediately. We do business with a lot of different companies so in the afternoon I do my best to visit as many customers as possible. Often I do overtime and then don't get home until late at night. It can be stressful.

To help reduce stress, we recently made a change in our office. Now we ask everyone to get to meetings on time. We also try to make a decision at the end of every meeting, so we don't need to repeat discussions.

I think most stress is in your own head. Personally, if I make a mistake, yes, I correct it, but I don't worry about it. If I leave work late, I always get a taxi home. But most days I get the train. At home my husband does the shopping and he does the housework. I don't have time for cleaning! One more thing: I do a lot of sport: especially swimming. Sport is the best cure for stress.

3 A dictionary gives useful information about words that go together. Look at the dictionary extracts. Do we use *make* or *do* with *arrangement* and *plan*?

> **arrangement** /əˈreɪndʒmənt/ **noun 1** [C, usually pl] plans or preparations for sth that will happen in the future: *Come round this evening and we'll* **make arrangements** *for the party.*
>
> **plan** /plæn/ **noun 1** [C] **a plan (for sth/to do sth)** an idea or arrangement for doing or achieving sth in the future: *We usually* **make** *our holiday* **plans** *in January.*

4 Work in pairs. Find other words in the text in **2** that go together with *make*, *do*, and *get*. Complete the word maps.

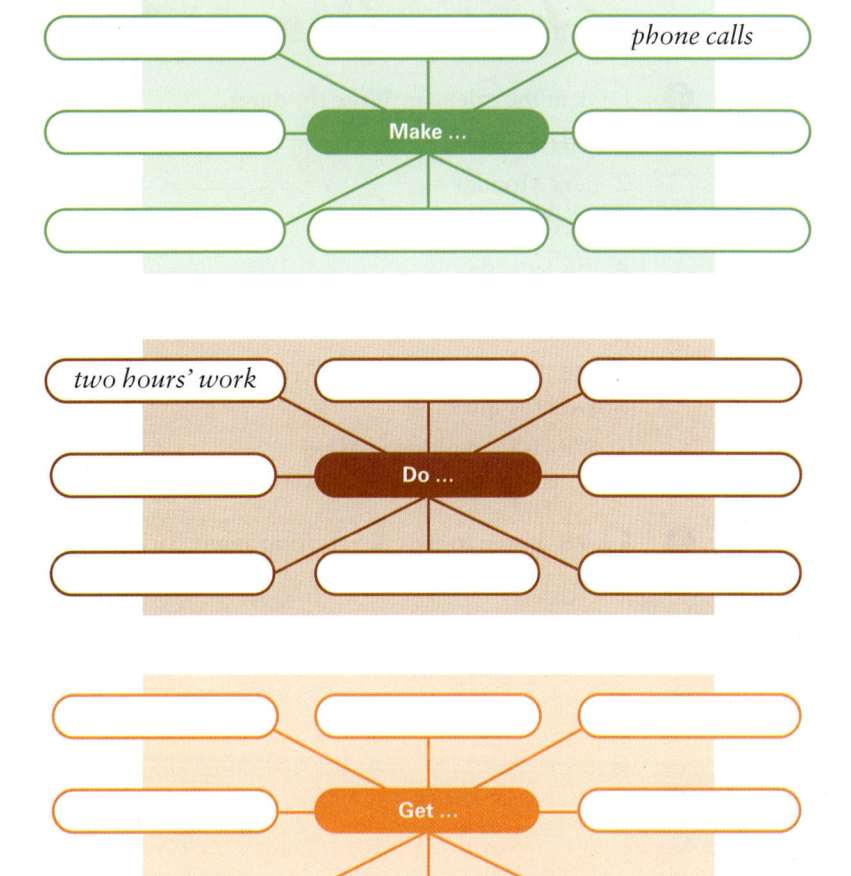

[Word map: **Make ...** with *phone calls* filled in, other bubbles empty]

[Word map: **Do ...** with *two hours' work* filled in, other bubbles empty]

[Word map: **Get ...** with *to work* filled in, other bubbles empty]

5 Look again at the word map of *get*. In which phrases does *get* mean:

1 arrive? _____
2 receive? _____
3 take? _____

6 Which of the activities in **4** do you do? How often do you do them?

Example *I sometimes make business trips.*
I never do overtime.

7 Work in pairs. Answer the questions.

1 When do you get stressed?
2 What is the best cure for stress?

UNIT 7 65

Focus on communication   **Making and changing arrangements**

	Wednesday	Thursday	Friday	Saturday	Sunday
August	1	2	3	4	5
Monday	Tuesday	Wednesday	Thursday	Friday	Saturday	Sunday
6	7	8	9	10	11	12
Monday	Tuesday	Wednesday	Thursday	Friday	Saturday	Sunday
13	14	15	16	17	18	19
Monday	Tuesday	Wednesday	Thursday	Friday	Saturday	Sunday
20	21	22	23	24	25	26
Monday	Tuesday	Wednesday	Thursday	Friday		
27	28	29	30	31		

1 Look at the calendar. Write the dates.
1. today — _8 August_
2. next Monday — _____
3. the day after tomorrow — _____
4. this Saturday — _____
5. the Sunday after next — _____

2 🎧 **7.5** Listen to a telephone conversation between two business colleagues. Answer the questions.
1. Why is Lara phoning Max?
2. When do they decide to meet?

3 🎧 **7.5** Listen to the conversation again. Tick (✓) the phrases you hear.

Making an arrangement	Saying 'yes'	Saying 'no'
Is … possible for you? ☐	… is OK. ☐	No, I'm sorry, I'm busy on … ☐
What about …? ☐	Yes, that's fine. ☐	No, … isn't possible. ☐
How about …? ☐		
See you on … , then. ☐		

66 ● UNIT 7

4 🎧 **7.5** Listen again and complete the sentences from the conversation.

M Yes, of course. How long ―――――――――¹?
L For a week. Is Tuesday possible for you?
M No, I'm sorry, I'm busy on Tuesday. ―――――――――² customers all day. What about Wednesday?
L No, that isn't possible. ―――――――――³ to a trade fair on Wednesday.

5 Look at the sentences in **4** and answer the questions.
1 Are Max and Lara talking about activities happening now or in the future?
2 When do we use the Present Continuous to talk about the future?

📘 **Pocket Book p.9**

6 Work in pairs. Practise making an arrangement. Use phrases from **3** and your own ideas.

A
- Hello, is that … ?
- It's … here. I'm phoning … … possible?
- No, I'm … How about … ?
- Good.
- Yes. See you …

B
- Yes, …
- No. I'm … What about …?
- Well, … isn't possible but … is OK.
- So …?

Telephoning tips

When you make arrangements to meet, repeat:
- the dates and times,
- all the details at the end of the conversation.

7 Change roles and practise the conversation again.

8 🎧 **7.6** Listen to the conversation and answer the questions.
1 Why is Lara phoning Max again?
2 What arrangement do they make?

9 🎧 **7.6** Listen again and complete the conversation.

M Hello, Max Cromer.
L Hello, Max. It's Lara. I'm very sorry but we've got a problem on Thursday. ―――――――――¹ the date of our meeting?
M Yes, of course. ―――――――――²?
L Well, any time on Friday or Monday afternoon is OK for us.
M Friday's ―――――――――³ because I'm flying to Brussels for the day. What about Monday afternoon?
L That's fine. What time ―――――――――⁴?
M Is 3.15 OK?
L Yes, ―――――――――⁵.
M Good. ―――――――――⁶ next Monday at 3.15, then.
L Thanks a lot, Max, and sorry again.
M That's no problem. Goodbye, Lara.

10 Work in pairs. Practise changing the appointment you made in **6**. Use phrases from **9** and your own ideas. Then change roles and practise again.

UNIT 7 • 67

UNIT 8
Relocating

AGENDA
- Future: *will*
- Future: *going to*
- Communications file
- Writing emails and faxes

Language focus 1

1 🎧 8.1 Work in pairs. Do the quizzes, then listen and check your answers.

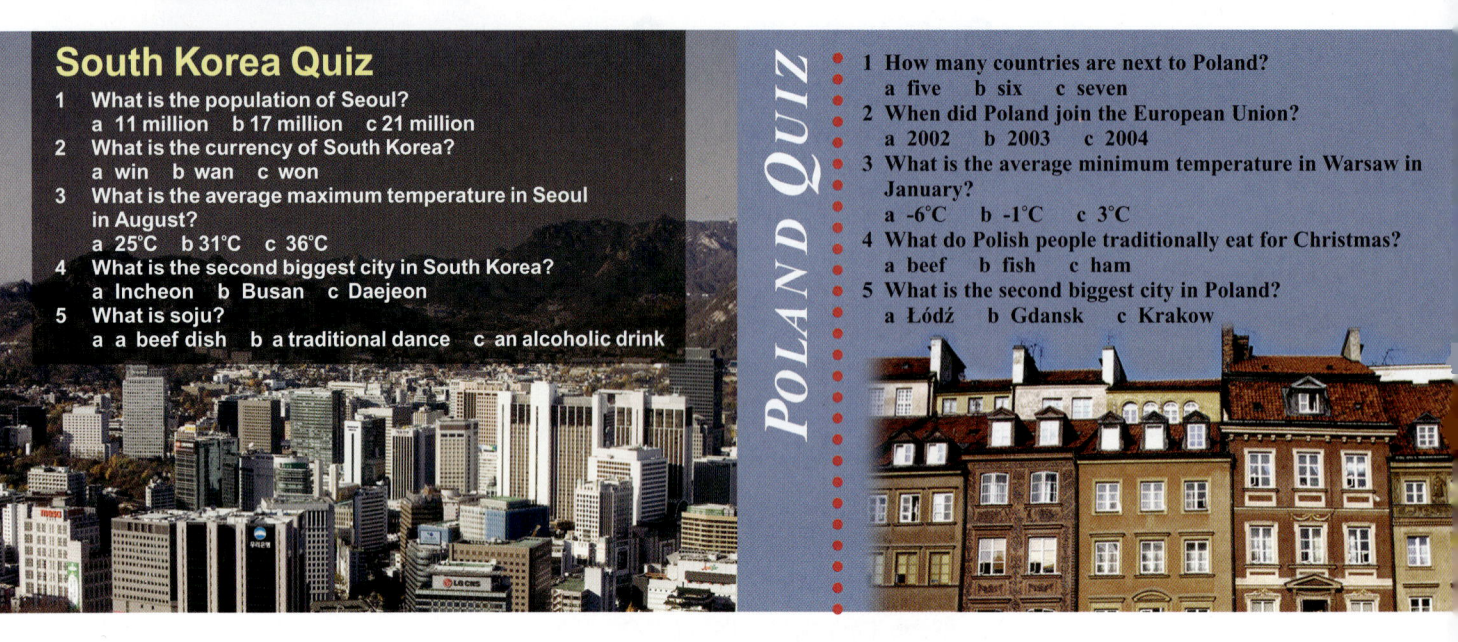

South Korea Quiz
1 What is the population of Seoul?
  a 11 million   b 17 million   c 21 million
2 What is the currency of South Korea?
  a win   b wan   c won
3 What is the average maximum temperature in Seoul in August?
  a 25°C   b 31°C   c 36°C
4 What is the second biggest city in South Korea?
  a Incheon   b Busan   c Daejeon
5 What is soju?
  a a beef dish   b a traditional dance   c an alcoholic drink

Poland Quiz
1 How many countries are next to Poland?
  a five   b six   c seven
2 When did Poland join the European Union?
  a 2002   b 2003   c 2004
3 What is the average minimum temperature in Warsaw in January?
  a -6°C   b -1°C   c 3°C
4 What do Polish people traditionally eat for Christmas?
  a beef   b fish   c ham
5 What is the second biggest city in Poland?
  a Łódź   b Gdansk   c Krakow

2 Read the letter to the *Europa* magazine website and answer the questions.
1 Where does Karol work?
2 Why is he going to Korea?
3 Why is he writing to *Europa* magazine?

Relocating to Korea
Karol Lazienki, 35, works in Warsaw

Dear Europa magazine,
Last month my company asked me to move to our head office in Seoul. The job will be for three years. Of course I said 'yes', immediately. I think it will be a great experience – and I won't get the same opportunity again. But now I need some advice. What will life be like in Korea?

3 On the *Europa* magazine website there is an interview with an expert on South Korea, Lee Jin. Match the questions 1–5 with Lee Jin's answers a–e.

1 What will his life be like?
2 Will it be difficult to meet people?
3 What kind of places will he go out to?
4 What is the food like?
5 What kind of questions will the ~~People in Korea~~ Koreans ask him?

a Delicious. But it's also very spicy so maybe he will need to be a little careful.
b They will ask 'Are you married?' 'How much do you earn?'
c It will be great. He will love it.
d Well, after work, he will probably go out to bars and restaurants with his colleagues.
e No! No, it won't. People in Korea are really friendly.

68 UNIT 8

4 🎧 **8.2** Listen to the interview and check your answers.

5 Look at the questions and answers in **3** again. Underline all the predictions. What verb do we use to predict future situations?

> ### Future: *will*
> Read the examples and grammar rules.
>
> **Positive**
> - Lots of people **will invite** him out.
>
> **Negative**
> - I **won't get** the same opportunity again.
>
> **Question**
> - Will they **ask** him personal questions?
> - Will it **be** difficult to meet people?
>
> **Short answer**
> Yes, they **will**.
> No, it **won't**.
>
> Note   'll = will   won't = will not
>
> - Use *will* to predict future situations and actions.
> - To make the *will* future, use *will* + infinitive.
>
> 📘 Pocket Book p.3

> ### Pronunciation
> We often contract *will* to *'ll* and *will not* to *won't*.
>
> 🎧 **8.3** Listen and repeat the sentences.
>
> 1 He'll come later.
> 2 You'll feel better soon.
> 3 She'll be here on Friday.
> 4 We'll get the news tomorrow.
> 5 It won't rain today.
> 6 You won't have any problems.
> 7 They won't be at the meeting.
> 8 I won't leave this evening.

Practice

1 🎧 **8.4** Next week, a Korean businesswoman, Kim Soo, has a business trip to Poland. She phones Karol Lazienki to ask some questions. Listen and complete the sentences.

1 I'm sure it _____ an interesting visit for you.
2 The weathermen say it _____ next week.
3 So I think you _____ sunglasses too.
4 _____ people _____ English?
5 Er … yes. I think so. Don't worry. You _____ any language problems.

2 Work in pairs. Ask and answer questions. Tick (✓) to show your partner's opinion.

Ask *Do you think you'll … ?*   Answer *Yes, I think so.*
                                            Maybe, I'm not sure.
                                            No, I don't think so.

Student A	Yes	Maybe	No	Student B	Yes	Maybe	No
1 buy something expensive next month?	☐	☐	☐	1 learn other languages in the future?	☐	☐	☐
2 improve your English a lot this year?	☐	☐	☐	2 work abroad in the next three years?	☐	☐	☐
3 change your job in the next two years?	☐	☐	☐	3 become very rich one day?	☐	☐	☐
4 take an exam in the future?	☐	☐	☐	4 have more than three children?	☐	☐	☐

Language focus 2

1 After Karol Lazienki moved to Seoul, *Europa* magazine interviewed him. Read the interview and answer the questions.

1 What is Karol going to do at work this week?
2 Where does Joo Dong-gun work?
3 What are they going to do tomorrow?
4 Is Karol going to visit Busan as a tourist?
5 What is Karol going to do in September?

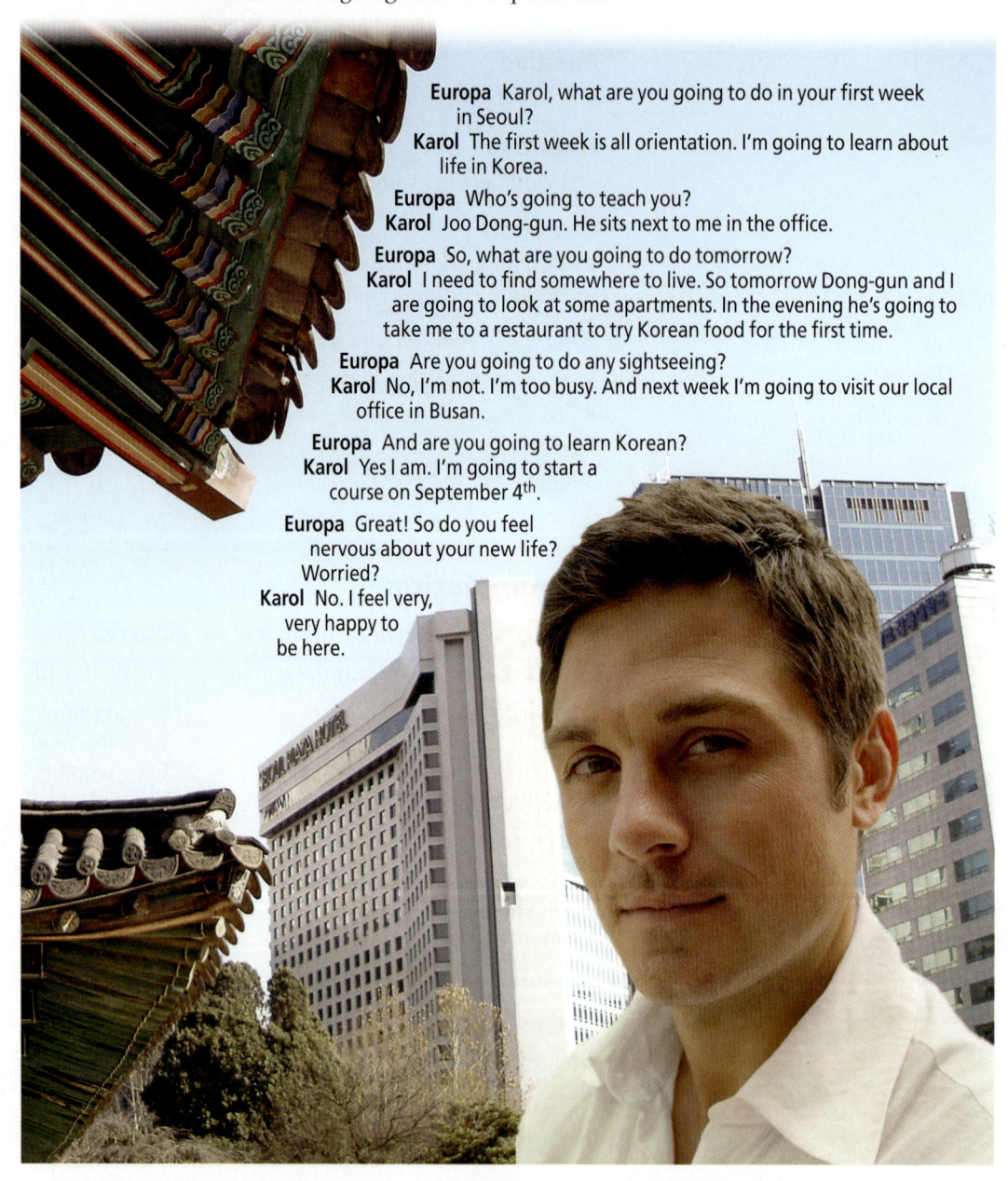

Europa Karol, what are you going to do in your first week in Seoul?
Karol The first week is all orientation. I'm going to learn about life in Korea.
Europa Who's going to teach you?
Karol Joo Dong-gun. He sits next to me in the office.
Europa So, what are you going to do tomorrow?
Karol I need to find somewhere to live. So tomorrow Dong-gun and I are going to look at some apartments. In the evening he's going to take me to a restaurant to try Korean food for the first time.
Europa Are you going to do any sightseeing?
Karol No, I'm not. I'm too busy. And next week I'm going to visit our local office in Busan.
Europa And are you going to learn Korean?
Karol Yes I am. I'm going to start a course on September 4th.
Europa Great! So do you feel nervous about your new life? Worried?
Karol No. I feel very, very happy to be here.

2 Look again at the interview in **1**. Find all the examples of Karol's future plans. What tense does he use for his future plans?

Future: *going to*

Read the examples and the grammar rules.

Positive
- Next week **I'm going to visit** our local office in Busan.

Negative
- **I'm not going to do** any sightseeing this week.

Question
- **Are** you **going to learn** Korean?
- **Are** you **going to do** any sightseeing?

Short answer
Yes, I am.
No, I'm not.

- Use *going to* to talk about future plans.
- To make the *going to* future, use *am/is/are going to* + infinitive.

Pocket Book p.3

70 UNIT 8

Practice

1 Dong-gun and Karol talked about their business trip to Busan. Look at Karol's notes and answer the questions.

1 What are they going to do on Monday afternoon?
2 Where are they going to have breakfast on Tuesday?
3 What are they going to do on Tuesday morning?
4 What are they going to do first on Tuesday afternoon?
5 Who are they going to meet on Monday evening?
6 Who are they going to talk to on Tuesday afternoon?

Trip to local office in Busan

Monday 28th
A.M. — Meet at airport
P.M. — Go to office in Busan. Speak to local staff
Evening — Dinner with regional manager

Tuesday 29th
A.M. — Breakfast hotel 7.00? 8.00?
Go to factory
14.00 — Give presentations:
  Dong-gun's presentation on company changes
  My presentation on Polish business
15.00 — Discussion with international sales team

2 Work in pairs. Ask and answer questions about your future plans. If you do not have any plans, say 'I don't know what I'm going to do'.

1 What are you going to do after this lesson?
2 What are you going to eat for dinner this evening?
3 What are you going to do at the weekend?
4 When is your English course going to finish?
5 What are you going to do after the course?

UNIT 8   71

Wordpower **Communications file**

1 Match the words and the pictures a to r.

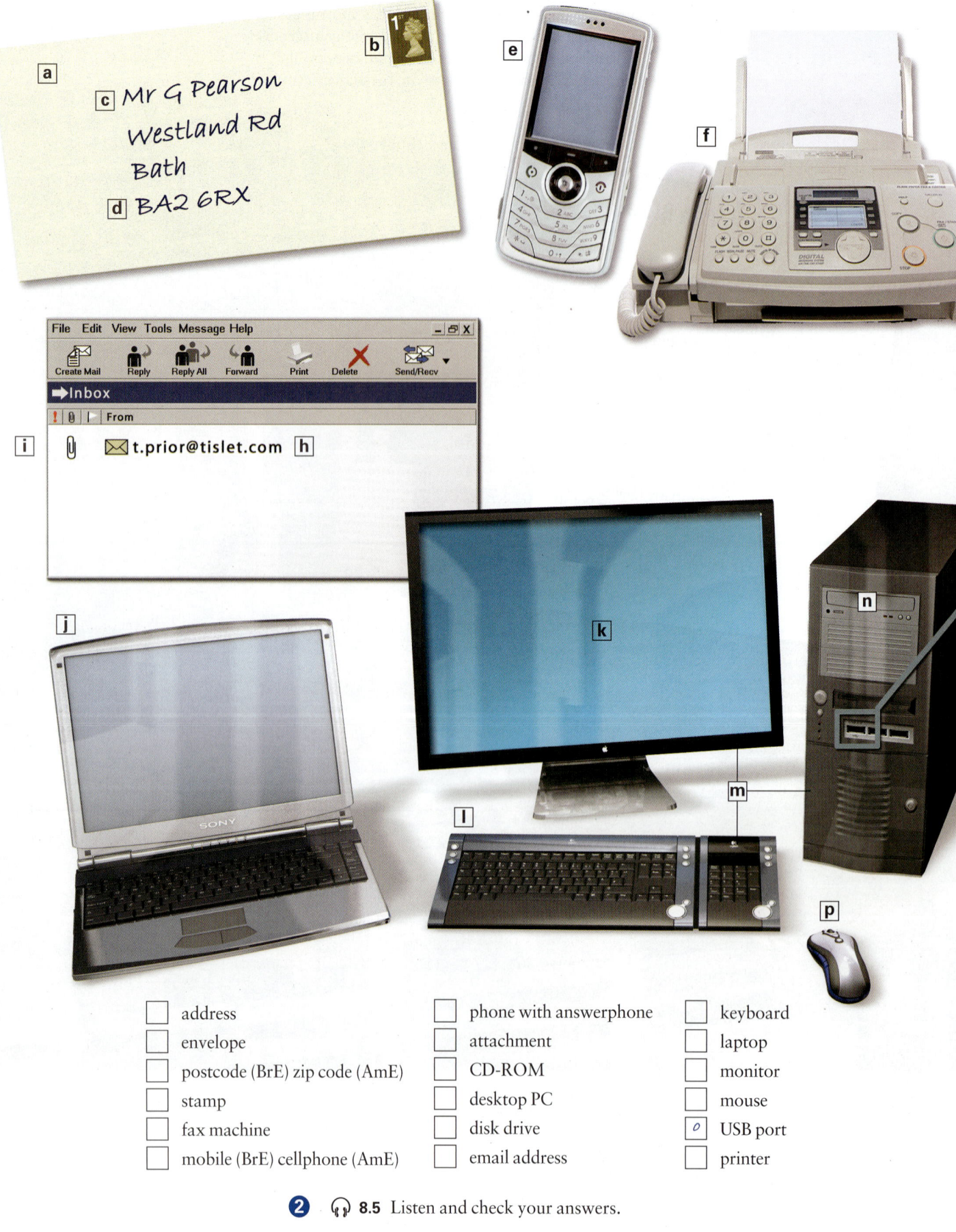

☐ address	☐ phone with answerphone	☐ keyboard
☐ envelope	☐ attachment	☐ laptop
☐ postcode (BrE) zip code (AmE)	☐ CD-ROM	☐ monitor
☐ stamp	☐ desktop PC	☐ mouse
☐ fax machine	☐ disk drive	☐ USB port (o)
☐ mobile (BrE) cellphone (AmE)	☐ email address	☐ printer

2 🎧 8.5 Listen and check your answers.

3 🎧 8.5 Listen again and repeat.

72 UNIT 8

4 Work in pairs. Test your partner on six words in **1**.

Example Student A *What's picture a?*
Student B *Envelope.*

5 🎧 **8.6** Listen and read the website and email addresses.

1 www.freeserve.net

The website is www dot freeserve dot net. That's freeserve, all one word, dot n-e-t.

2 j_ellis@dialstart.co.uk

My email address is j underscore ellis That's e double-l i-s at dialstart, that's d-i-a-l-s-t-a-r-t dot co dot uk.

3 timflan@aol.com

My email address is timflan. That's all one word, t-i-m-f-l-a-n at a-o-l dot com.

6 🎧 **8.7** Listen and write the website and email addresses.

1 _____
2 _____
3 _____
4 _____
5 _____

7 Work in groups. Look at the words in the box below. Decide which method of communication is:

a the cheapest
b the most expensive
c the fastest
d the slowest
e the most reliable
f the most unreliable
g the most frustrating
h the best way of keeping information a long time
i the best way to send complicated information
j the best way of communicating with friends
k the best way of communicating with your colleagues

| answerphone message | email | fax | letter |
| phone call | post-it note | text message | visiting in person |

UNIT 8   73

Focus on communication   **Writing emails and faxes**

1 Do you write emails or faxes in English?
　　1 Who do you write to?　　3 Do you write anything in English?
　　2 What do you write about?　　4 What problems do you have writing in English?

2 Read the emails and faxes a–e. Which email or fax:
　　1 gives the date of a meeting?　　4 asks for more information?
　　2 confirms an arrangement?　　5 gives bad news?
　　3 is an invitation?

a

Lynch Carlson Ltd.
Newton Industrial park   London   SE1 2TA   Tel 020 7645 7800   Fax: 020 7645 7804

To:　　Mr L Hunt, Omicron
Date:　　30 January

Dear Mr Hunt

Thank you for your fax of 29 January. I am sorry to inform you that we no longer produce Model 671. However, Models 679 and 683 are similar and may meet your requirements.

Please contact us again if you would like further information.

Yours sincerely

J. Banner

J. Banner (Ms)
Customer Services

c

03 76 06 681 13 49

SETEX S.p.A
Via Porto Vecchio 32, Roma, 00185   Tel. 06-681-11-43   Fax. 06-684-73-4

FAX MESSAGE　　　　No. of pages : 　2

To:　　Sophie Masset
From:　　Aldo Marino
Date:　　10 September

This fax is to confirm your visit on 17 September, arriving at 9.45 a.m. I apologize for the change of plans and hope this does not cause any problems. A map of how to get here follows on page 2. Looking forward to meeting you next week.

Regards
Aldo

b

Subject:　Hello!

Dear Jamie

This email is to get in touch again – after a very long time! How are you? How's the new job going? I'd love to see you again soon. How about coming to stay with us one weekend next month, if you can find the time?

We had a great holiday in Canada and we've got lots of photos to show you!

Hoping to see you soon.

Love
Robin

Pocket Book p.19

74　UNIT 8

3 Complete the table with phrases from the emails and faxes.

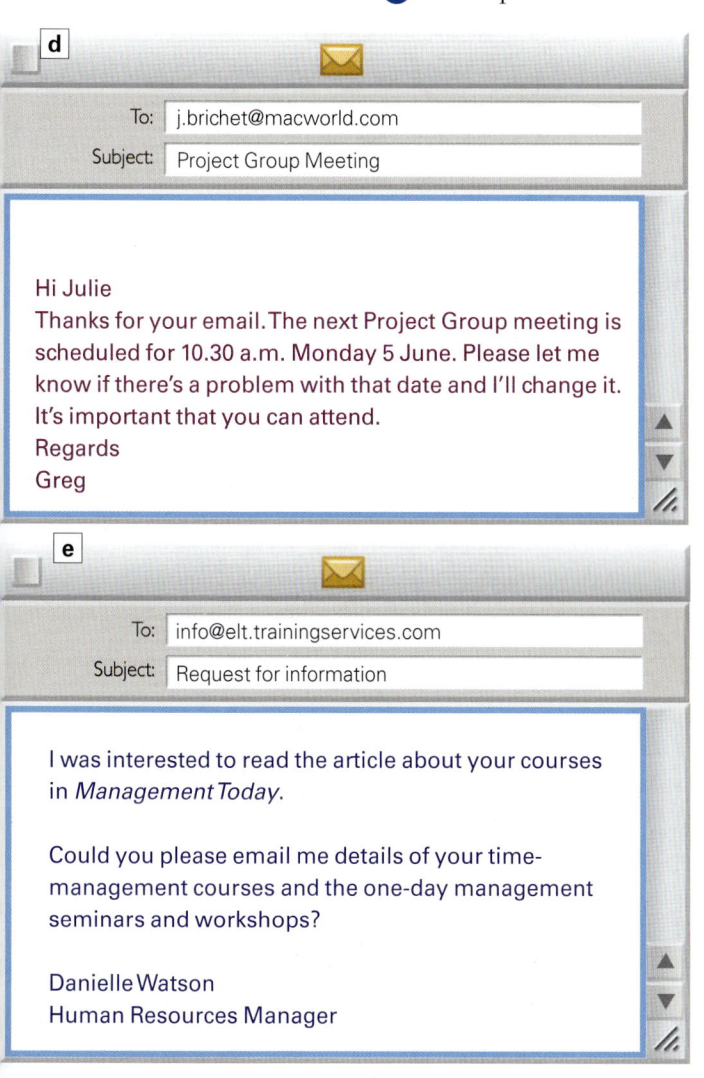

d

To: j.brichet@macworld.com
Subject: Project Group Meeting

Hi Julie
Thanks for your email. The next Project Group meeting is scheduled for 10.30 a.m. Monday 5 June. Please let me know if there's a problem with that date and I'll change it. It's important that you can attend.
Regards
Greg

e

To: info@elt.trainingservices.com
Subject: Request for information

I was interested to read the article about your courses in *Management Today*.

Could you please email me details of your time-management courses and the one-day management seminars and workshops?

Danielle Watson
Human Resources Manager

Starting
Following your phone call (*today* …)
Thank you ——————— (*of 29 January*)
——————— your email

Saying why you're writing
I am writing (*to tell you that* …)
I am pleased (*to tell you that* …)
——————— (*to confirm your visit* …)
——————— (*to get in touch again.*)

Requesting
——————— (*details of* …)
Would you please email me (*a list of* …)
Please fax me (*your price list* …)
Please ——————— (*if there's a problem* …)

Giving bad news
——————— (*to inform you* …)
Unfortunately …

Apologizing
——————— (*the change of plans*)
Sorry about (*the mistake*)

Ending
Please ——————— (*if you would like further information*)
——————— (*meeting you next week*)
——————— (*to see you soon*)

4 Complete the email below. Use phrases from the table in **3**. Write your address and your name at the end.

To: info@studyworldwide.org.uk
Subject: Study in the UK information pack

… a list of language schools in London which offer two or four-week intensive English for Business courses. I would like to do a course of this type in the autumn. My address is …

5 Continue this email to a colleague who was ill and did not come to the last English lesson. Tell him/her what you studied in the lesson and what homework you had. Write the email address.

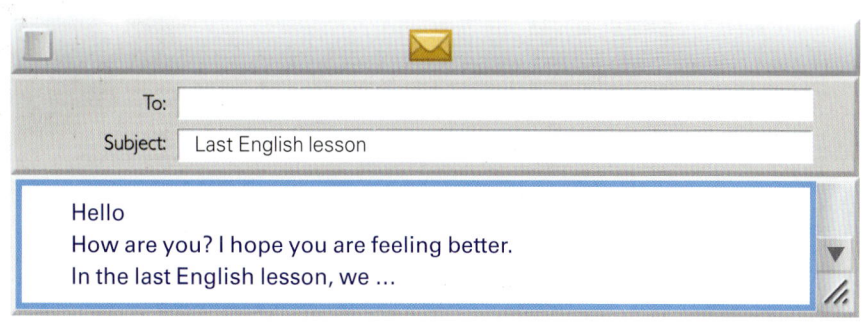

To:
Subject: Last English lesson

Hello
How are you? I hope you are feeling better.
In the last English lesson, we …

UNIT 8   75

REVIEW UNIT D

▼ AGENDA
▶ Grammar ❶ – ❸
▶ Vocabulary ❹
▶ Communication ❺, ❻

This unit reviews the main language points from Units 7 and 8. Complete the exercises. Check your learning with the self-check box at the end.

❶ Present Simple and Present Continuous

Complete the sentences. Write the Present Simple or Present Continuous form of the verb in brackets.

1 John _____ for Microsoft. He started there ten years ago. (work)
2 This week they _____ our office in Vietnam (visit).
3 This year unemployment in my country _____ (go up).
4 People in the company _____ work at 7 a.m. (start).
5 Where _____ you _____ (live)? – Tokyo. I come from Japan.
6 More and more people _____ their holidays (not take).

❷ Future: *will*

Work in pairs. Ask and answer questions.
Answer *Yes, definitely./Yes, I think so./Maybe. I'm not sure./No, I don't think so.*

In your working life do you think you'll:

1 change jobs more than three times?
2 study to get another qualification?
3 spend more than six months working in another country?
4 start your own company?
5 work freelance?

❸ Future: *going to*

Work in pairs. Look at the screen of Sezen Rifat's personal organizer. Make sentences with *going to* to describe her plans.

❹ Vocabulary: *do* and *make*

Work in pairs. Which words do we use with *make*? Which do we use with *do*?

> homework
> a decision
> a phone call
> a mistake
> the housework
> some work
> a business trip
> an appointment
> business (with someone)
> the shopping
> a sport
> a change

• Ask Bob about his plans for the Asia sales team.
• Phone Tokyo office to arrange visit for next month.
• Buy souvenirs for Japanese customers.
• Learn some phrases to introduce myself in Japanese.
• Get some guide books and plan a trip for day off.

76 ● REVIEW UNIT D

5 Telephoning: making and changing arrangements

Work in pairs. Complete the telephone conversations. Write ONE word in each gap. (*I'm* = one word.)

Conversation 1
P Hello, _____ _____¹ Susie Denver?
S Yes, _____².
P Susie, it's Paolo. I'm _____³ to arrange a meeting. Are _____ _____⁴ on Wednesday next week?
S No, I'm _____⁵, I'm flying to Brussels on Wednesday. What _____⁶ Thursday?
P Thursday morning isn't _____⁷ because I'm visiting some customers but the afternoon is _____⁸. Shall we _____⁹ 3 o'clock?
S Yes. So, 3 o'clock on Thursday, in Room 10?
P Fine. See you next week, Susie. Bye.

Conversation 2
P Hello, Paolo Aldrini.
S Hello, Paolo. _____¹ Susie. I'm very _____² but I've got a problem. Some important visitors are coming on Thursday. _____³ we _____⁴ the date of our meeting?
P Yes, of course. When are you _____⁵?
S Well, any time on Friday is _____⁶ for me.
P How _____⁷ just after lunch, say 2.15?
S That's _____⁸.
P Good. _____ _____⁹ on Friday, at 2.15, then.
S _____¹⁰ Paolo, and sorry again.
P That's no problem. Bye, Susie.

6 Writing emails and faxes

1 Match A and B to make typical sentences for faxes and emails.

A	B
1 Thank you for	a see you again soon.
2 Could you please	b your fax of 4 March.
3 Hoping to	c the mistake in our brochure.
4 Please let me know if	d your email.
5 I am writing	e tell you how to get to the hotel.
6 I apologize for	f send me a copy of your brochure?
7 Thanks for	g that prices will increase by 20%.
8 Looking forward to	h to inform you of our new address.
9 This email is to	i you cannot come on that date.
10 I am sorry to inform you	j meeting you at the next conference.

2 Match the sentences in 6.1 to the headings.

Starting _____ Giving bad news _____
Saying why you're writing _____ Apologizing _____
Requesting _____ Ending _____

Look at the self-check box. Tick the areas you need to review again.

SELF-CHECK BOX	Yes	No	Pocket Book
• Present Simple and Present Continuous			11, 9
• Future: *will*			3
• Future: *going to*			3
• Vocabulary: *do* and *make*			
• Telephoning: making and changing arrangements			15
• Writing emails and faxes			19

REVIEW UNIT D 77

UNIT 9
Destination with a difference

▼ AGENDA
- Modal verbs: *should/shouldn't, may, can/can't, have to/don't have to*
- Hotel file
- Invitations
- Suggestions

Language focus

1 Read the first part of a newspaper article. What is the article about?

Great escapes

Are you bored with the same old vacation? If you are, you should try a new kind of holiday and spend your break in prison: a prison converted into a hotel. It sounds strange, but in the world of tourism, businesses have to be innovative. Today we look at two very unusual hotels.

2 Work in pairs and look at the pictures. What are the differences between the prison cell and the hotel room?

3 Read the rest of the article *Great escapes*. Answer the questions.
1 Where are the two hotels?
2 Which room at Malmaison is the most expensive?
3 Which parts of Malmaison look like a prison?
4 Which parts of Hostel Celica look like a prison?
5 What special events happen at Hostel Celica?

★★ Europa*Magazine*

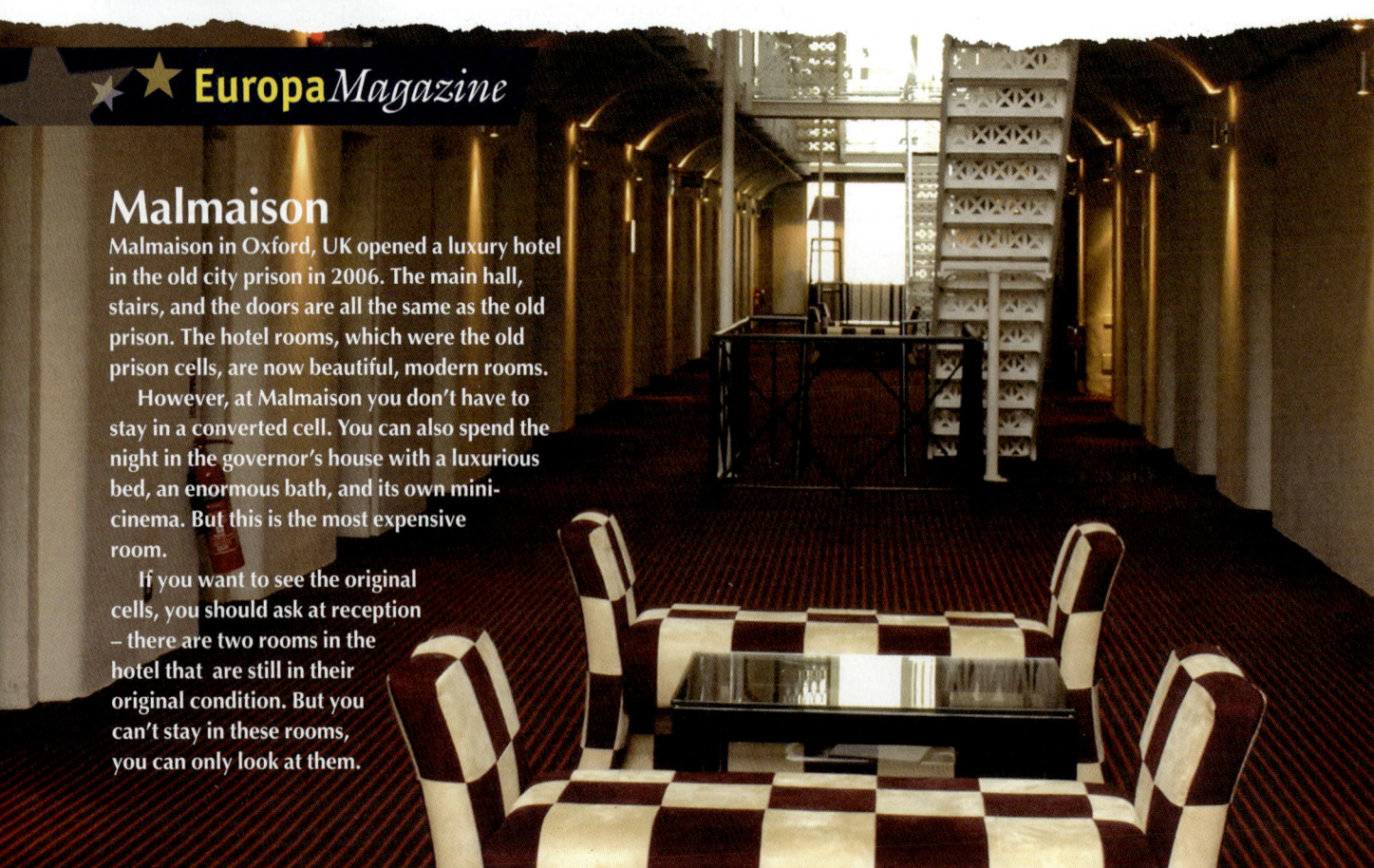

Malmaison

Malmaison in Oxford, UK opened a luxury hotel in the old city prison in 2006. The main hall, stairs, and the doors are all the same as the old prison. The hotel rooms, which were the old prison cells, are now beautiful, modern rooms.

However, at Malmaison you don't have to stay in a converted cell. You can also spend the night in the governor's house with a luxurious bed, an enormous bath, and its own mini-cinema. But this is the most expensive room.

If you want to see the original cells, you should ask at reception – there are two rooms in the hotel that are still in their original condition. But you can't stay in these rooms, you can only look at them.

4 Work in pairs. You can spend a weekend at Hostel Celica or Malmaison. Decide which hotel you will stay in.

Modal verbs: should/shouldn't, may, can/can't, have to/don't have to

Read the examples and answer the questions.

It's a good idea
- You **should** try a new kind of holiday.

It's not a good idea
- You **shouldn't** leave money or valuables in your room.

It's possible
- You **can** stay in a private room.
- You don't know who **may** be in the hotel.

It's not possible
- You **can't** stay in these rooms.

It's necessary
- You **have to** take all the sheets off your bed when you leave.

It's not necessary
- You **don't have to** stay in a converted cell.

Find other sentences with *should*, *can*, and *have to* in the article.

How do we make questions with *should* and *can*?

How do we make questions with *have to*?

Pocket Book p.6

Pronunciation

1 9.1 Listen to the examples. How do you pronounce *can* and *can't*?
   a You can stay in a private room.
   b You can't make a prison into a hotel!

2 9.2 Listen. Write *a* if you hear *can*, or *b* if you hear *can't*.
   1 ____   3 ____   5 ____   7 ____
   2 ____   4 ____   6 ____   8 ____

3 9.2 Listen again and repeat.

Hostel Celica

You don't have to spend a lot of money to stay in a prison hotel. Hostel Celica in Ljubljana, Slovenia, was once a military prison and now it is a youth hostel. You can stay in a private room or a seven-person apartment. All the apartments are newly decorated in a stylish, modern way.

But at this hostel, you can't escape the hotel's history. Guests can see graffiti on the prison walls, and the windows and doors have bars. You also have to take all the sheets off your bed when you leave!

For entertainment, the hotel has music concerts and art exhibitions. It is also right in the city centre if you want to escape to Ljubljana's shops and restaurants. And remember: you shouldn't leave money or valuables in your room. You don't know who may be in the hotel …

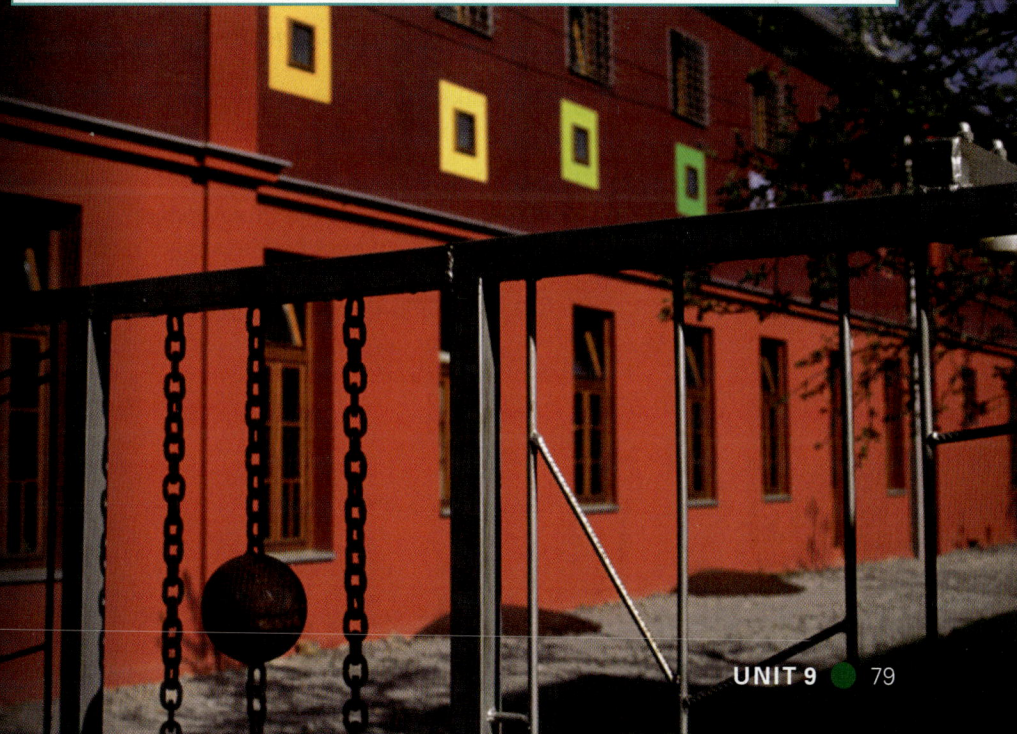

UNIT 9   79

Practice

1 Complete the sentences about Hostel Celica and Malmaison, Oxford. Use the correct modal verb, *should/shouldn't, can/can't, have to/don't have to*.

1 You *don't have to* fly to Ljubljana (it's not necessary). You _____ also get there by train (it's possible).
2 You _____ go in August (it's not a good idea) because all the rooms in the hotel may be booked up.
3 You _____ sleep in the old prison building (it's not necessary). You _____ book the governor's room if you prefer (it's possible).
4 You _____ eat out in Ljubljana (it's a good idea) – the restaurants are fantastic!
5 At Hostel Celica you _____ pay for bed and breakfast when you arrive (it's necessary) and you _____ bring pets into the hotel (it's not possible).

2 Work in pairs. Ask and answer questions. Note your partner's answers.

Ask *Do you have to …?*   Answer *Yes, I do./No, I don't.*

	My partner's answers	
At work	Yes	No
1 wear formal clothes?	☐	☐
2 speak English on the phone?	☐	☐
3 use a computer?	☐	☐
4 look after visitors?	☐	☐
5 travel a lot?	☐	☐
6 work at weekends?	☐	☐
At home		
1 cook?	☐	☐
2 study?	☐	☐
3 do the housework?	☐	☐
4 do the shopping?	☐	☐
5 look after children?	☐	☐
6 do the gardening?	☐	☐

3 Tell the class three things about your partner.

Example *My partner has to …, but he/she doesn't have to …*

4 Make true sentences about yourself. Underline the positive or negative form and complete the sentence with your reason.

Example *I should/shouldn't do more sport because I want to get fit.*

1 I *can/can't* go out this evening …
2 I *have to/don't have to* study English at the weekend …
3 I *should/shouldn't* work longer hours …
4 I *can/can't* have a holiday next month …
5 I *have to/don't have to* get more exercise …
6 I *should/shouldn't* learn another language …

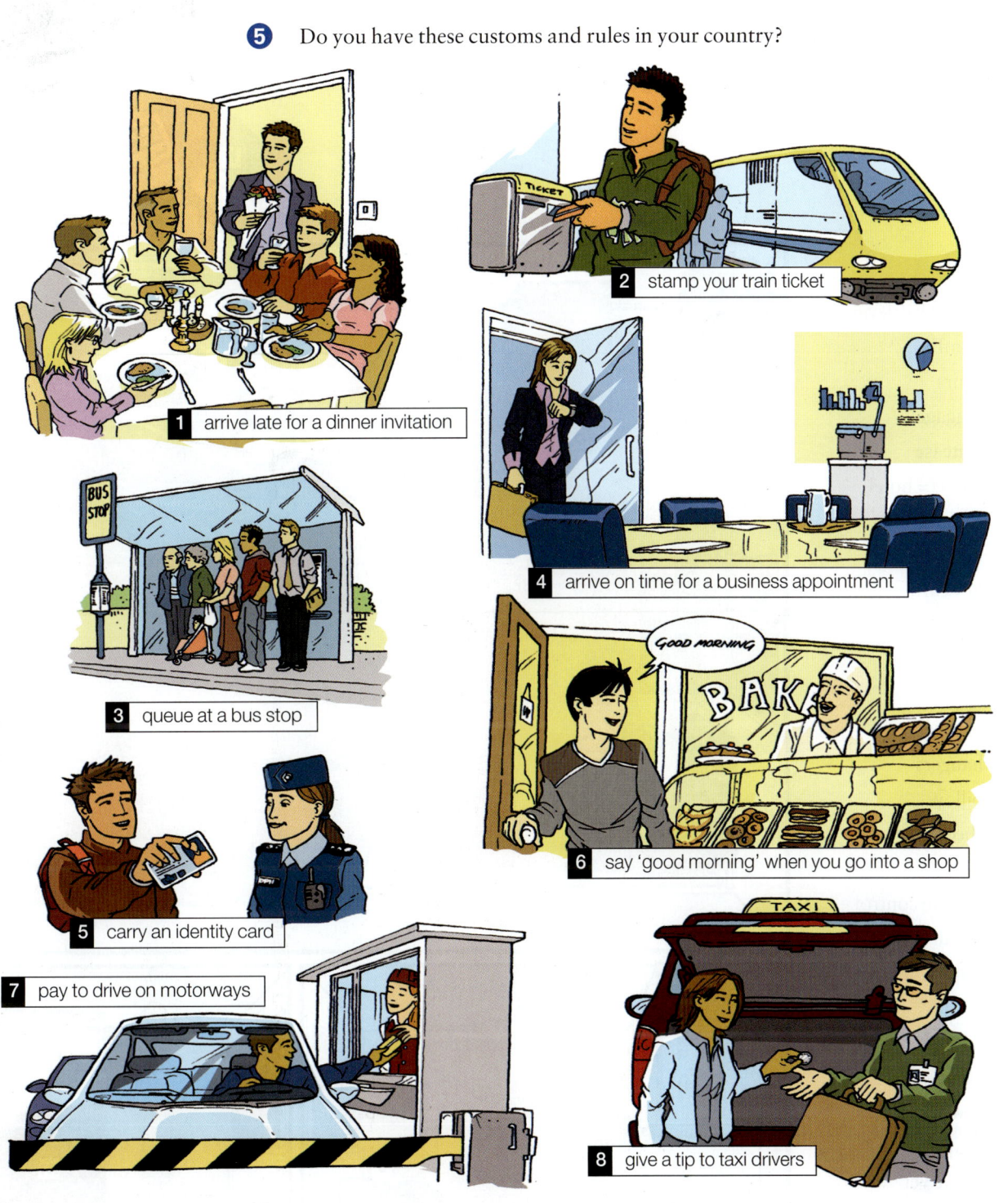

5 Do you have these customs and rules in your country?

1 arrive late for a dinner invitation
2 stamp your train ticket
3 queue at a bus stop
4 arrive on time for a business appointment
5 carry an identity card
6 say 'good morning' when you go into a shop
7 pay to drive on motorways
8 give a tip to taxi drivers

6 Work in pairs. Imagine your partner is a foreign visitor to your country. Give him/her advice about the customs and rules in the pictures.

Use *should/shouldn't*, *have to/don't have to*.

Example *You have to carry an identity card with you.*

7 What other advice can you give a foreign visitor to your country?

8 Work in groups. What advice can you give about visiting other countries? Prepare a list of *Tips for international travellers*. Your tips can be serious or funny. Choose from these topics.
- Meeting people
- Eating and drinking
- Travelling
- Tipping
- Queuing
- Clothes

UNIT 9　81

Wordpower

Hotel file

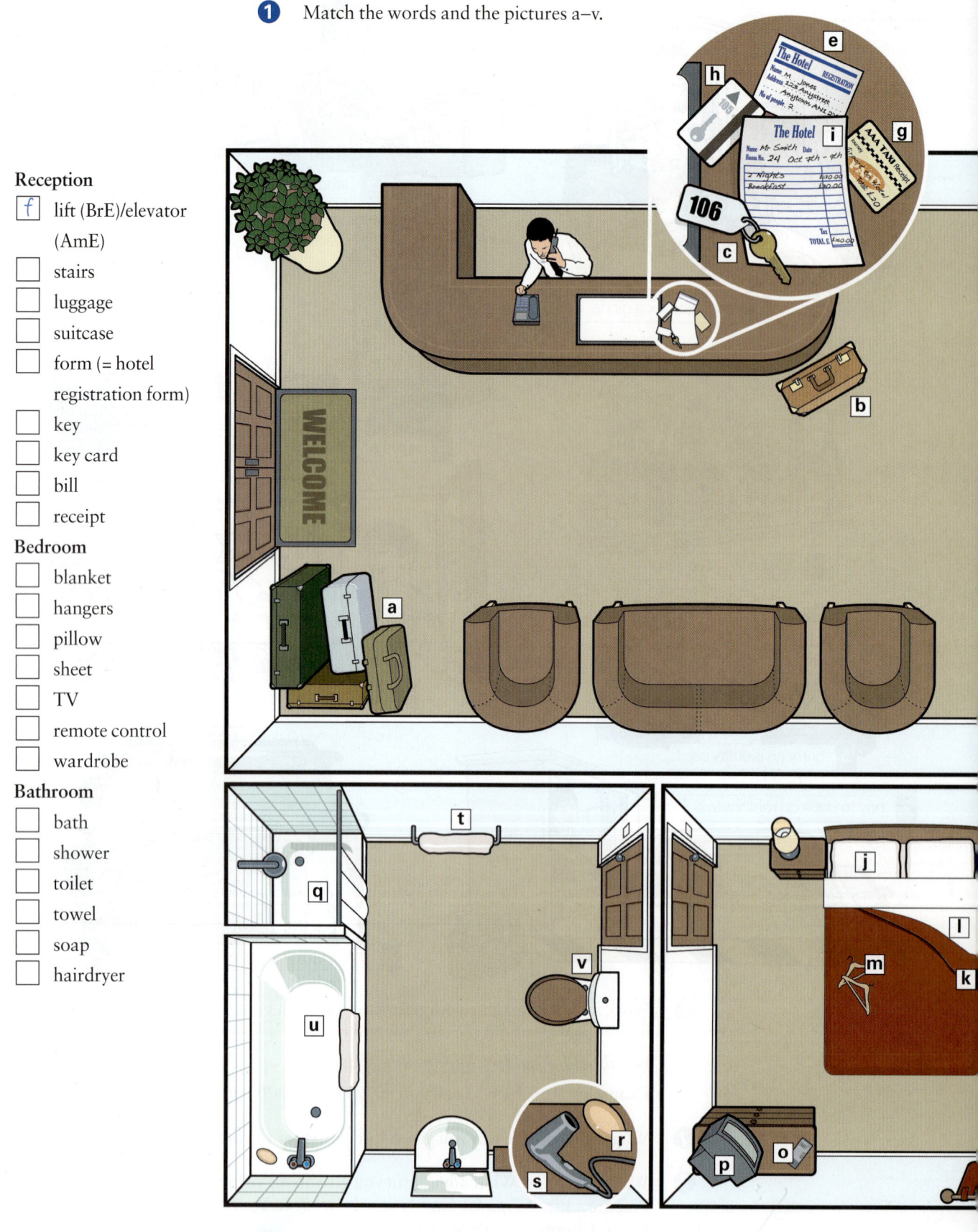

1 Match the words and the pictures a–v.

Reception
- [f] lift (BrE)/elevator (AmE)
- [ ] stairs
- [ ] luggage
- [ ] suitcase
- [ ] form (= hotel registration form)
- [ ] key
- [ ] key card
- [ ] bill
- [ ] receipt

Bedroom
- [ ] blanket
- [ ] hangers
- [ ] pillow
- [ ] sheet
- [ ] TV
- [ ] remote control
- [ ] wardrobe

Bathroom
- [ ] bath
- [ ] shower
- [ ] toilet
- [ ] towel
- [ ] soap
- [ ] hairdryer

2 🎧 9.3 Listen and check your answers.

3 Work in pairs. Test your partner on the words in ①. Give a description but do not give the word.

Example   Student A *You get this when you pay your hotel bill.*
          Student B *A receipt.*

82 ● UNIT 9

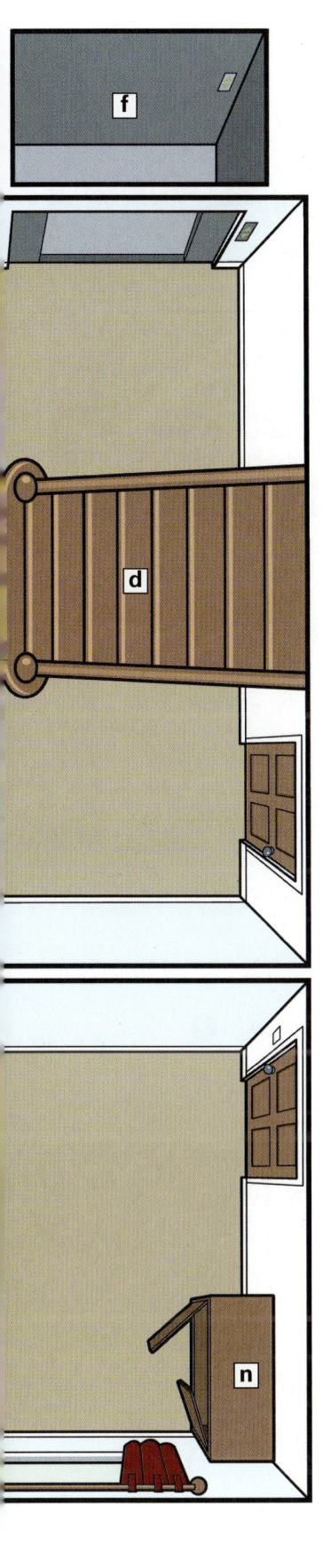

4 🎧 9.4 Listen to six short conversations. Match each conversation 1–6 with a picture a–f.

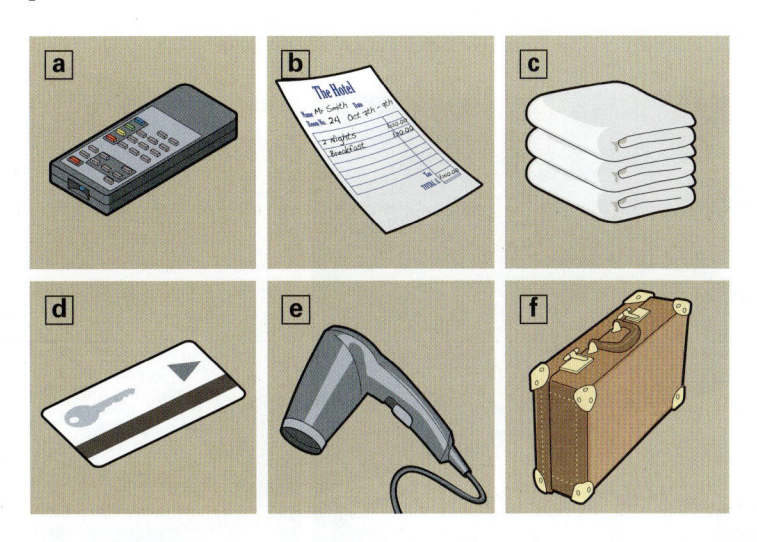

5 🎧 9.4 Listen to the six short conversations again. In each conversation, what does the guest want?

6 Work in pairs. Read some comments from hotel guests. What are the people talking about?

"**They**'re too heavy to carry."

"I need **it** to show to my boss, because my company is paying for the hotel."

"There are only **two** in the wardrobe and we have lots of clothes."

"It's cold today. I need another **one** on my bed."

"I don't have time for **one**. I'll have a shower instead."

"I put **it** in the lock, but it doesn't work."

"He doesn't want to walk up **them**, because he has to carry his suitcases."

"I always sleep with **two** under my head, but the bed only has one."

"Every guest has to complete **this** when they check into the hotel."

UNIT 9 83

Focus on communication

Invitations

1 🎧 **9.5** Listen to four conversations. Match the conversations and pictures.

a ☐

b ☐

2 🎧 **9.5** Listen again. Tick (✓) the phrases you hear.

Inviting	Saying 'yes'	Saying 'no' + reason
Would you like to (visit …)? ☐	Thank you. That would be interesting. ☐	Thanks for asking me, but I'm afraid (I've got something planned). ☐
Would you have (dinner) with me …? ☐	Thank you very much. I'd enjoy that. ☐	I'd love to, but unfortunately (I have to …). ☐
How about (a trip to …)? ☐	That's a good idea. ☐	I'm sorry, but (I'll be away …). ☐
What about (doing)? ☐		

📘 **Pocket Book p.15**

3 Work in pairs. Make and reply to invitations. Use the phrases in **2**. Give a reason when you don't accept.

STUDENT A

Conversation 1
Student B is visiting your company.
Invite him/her to
1 have dinner with you this evening.
2 go to the theatre on Friday evening.
3 visit the company's new offices.
4 go to London on Saturday.

STUDENT B

Conversation 1
You are visiting Student A's company.
1 Say yes.
2 Say no.
3 Say yes.
4 Say no.

STUDENT B

Conversation 2
Student A is visiting your company.
Invite him/her to
1 have lunch with you and your colleagues.
2 see a presentation of the company's new products.
3 have dinner at your house tomorrow evening.
4 visit some local places of interest at the weekend.

STUDENT A

Conversation 2
You are visiting Student B's company.
1 Say no.
2 Say yes.
3 Say yes.
4 Say no.

84 ● UNIT 9

Suggestions

1 🎧 **9.6** Listen to four conversations. Tick (✓) to show if the people accept the suggestion or not.

Conversation	Yes	No
1 Bob	☐	☐
2 Renzo	☐	☐
3 Michelle	☐	☐
4 Lara	☐	☐

2 🎧 **9.6** Listen again. Tick (✓) the phrases you hear.

Suggesting	Saying 'yes'	Saying 'no' + reason
How about (*playing* ...)? ☐	That's a good idea. ☐	That's a good idea, but (*I have to* ...). ☐
What about (*coming*...)? ☐	Great idea. ☐	Sorry, I can't. (*I'm going* ...). ☐
Why don't we (*go* ...)? ☐	OK. Fine. ☐	I'd love to, but (*my mother* ...). ☐
Let's (*go* ...). ☐		

📗 Pocket Book p.16

3 Work in pairs. Make and reply to suggestions about ways to improve your English outside the classroom. Use the phrases in **2**.

Example *study English together*
A *How about studying English together outside the classroom?*
B *That's a good idea, but the problem is how to find the time!*

Suggest you

1 help each other with the homework.
2 start a library of books in easy English.
3 watch English films on video.
4 create your own mini-dictionary of useful words.
5 plan a language-study holiday in the UK or USA.

Add four more ideas of your own.

4 Walk around the class. Make invitations and suggestions to other students (e.g. for evening/weekend activities). Reply to invitations and suggestions from other students.

Don't forget!
- use the *-ing* verb form after *How about ...?* and *What about ...?*
- use the verb without *to* after *Why don't we...?*
- give a reason when you don't accept a suggestion.

UNIT 10
Developing a company

▼ AGENDA
- Past Simple and Present Perfect
- Verbs with prepositions
- Answerphone messages ℓ
- Emails and mobile phones

Language focus

1 Match the pictures with the names of outdoor sports.

a b c d e

mountain climbing   hiking   snowboarding
long-distance running   skiing

What kind of clothes and equipment do people need for these outdoor sports? Can you name any sportswear companies?

2 Read about *The North Face* sportswear company. There are five facts which are incorrect. What do you think they are?

The North Face

Two hikers founded *The North Face* in Holland in 1966. They chose the company name because the 'north face' of a mountain is the easiest to climb. Three years later the company began designing its own brand of climbing clothes and equipment, and in the 1980s the company started producing clothes for football.

By 1989 *The North Face* offered a collection of outdoor wear, ski wear, sleeping bags, packs, and tents. In 2000 *The North Face* designed more products for rock climbers, backpackers, and people who enjoy the outdoors. In spring 1999 it started its own range of trekking and running shoes.

The North Face works with some amazing sportsmen and women. Dean Karnazes, who ran a marathon to the North Pole in running shoes in 2002, helps *The North Face* develop their running footwear and equipment.

🎧 **10.1** Listen and correct the facts.

3 Match the words with the definitions.

A	B
1 to sponsor	a a person who competes in a sport
2 a range	b a journey, often to a place that is not well known
3 to expand	c to support a project by giving money
4 an expedition	d a variety of products that people can buy
5 an athlete	e to become bigger

4 🎧 **10.2** Listen to a discussion about *The North Face*'s business. Complete the information.

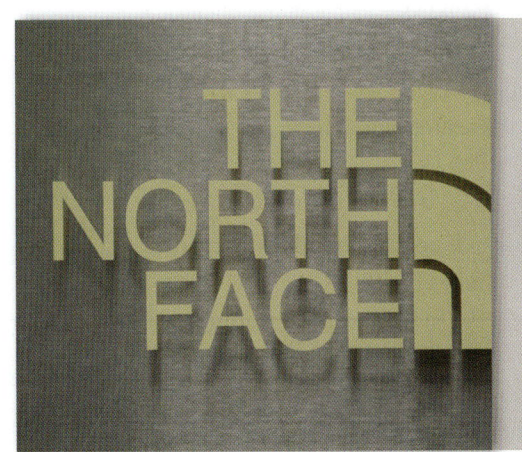

1 Originally their products were for _____ and _____.
2 They have recently introduced a range of designer _____ and _____.
3 Since 1969 they have also sponsored _____.
4 Kit DesLauriers climbed _____ and _____ down from the summit.
5 It has kept its _____.

5 Work in pairs. Can you think of other companies who have developed in a similar way to *The North Face*?

Past Simple and Present Perfect

Read the examples and the grammar rules.

Past Simple

- Two hikers **founded** *The North Face* in 1966.
- In the 1980s the company **started** producing ski wear.

Use the Past Simple to talk about an event at a particular time in the past. We often use time phrases such as: *in 1996, five years ago, last week.*

Present Perfect

- Their range of products **has expanded** a lot.

  Use the Present Perfect to talk about an event that starts in the past and may continue in the future.

- They **have** recently **introduced** a range of designer coats and jackets.

We also use the Present Perfect to talk about an event in the past which has a connection to the present. We do not refer to the exact time the event happened.

- To make the Present Perfect use *has* or *'s/have* or *'ve* + Past Participle (e.g. *decided, sold*).

ever

Have you **ever bought** a *North Face* product?
Yes, I **have**.
Have you **ever used** these for hiking or climbing?
No, I **haven't**.

Use the Present Perfect with *ever* to ask if an event happened at any time in the past. Do not use *ever* in the answer.

📘 Pocket Book p.10

Past Participles

The Past Participle of regular verbs is the same as the Past Simple form.

Infinitive	Past Simple	Past Participle
change	changed	changed
produce	produced	produced

The Past Participle of irregular verbs is sometimes the same as the Past Simple form and sometimes different.

Infinitive	Past Simple	Past Participle
buy	bought	bought
grow	grew	grown

📘 Pocket Book p.20

Pronunciation

1 🎧 **10.3** Listen and repeat the sentences.

1 a I've finished the work.
  b I finished the work.

2 a He's solved the problem.
  b He solved the problem.

2 🎧 **10.4** Listen and tick (✓) the sentence you hear, a or b.

1 a We've travelled a lot.
  b We travelled a lot.

2 a He's changed his job.
  b He changed his job.

3 a I've corrected the mistake.
  b I corrected the mistake.

4 a They've invited us to dinner.
  b They invited us to dinner.

5 a I've found my passport.
  b I found my passport.

6 a It's stopped raining.
  b It stopped raining.

3 🎧 **10.5** Listen and repeat the sentences in **2** above.

Practice

1 Some sentences are not correct. Correct them using the Past Simple or Present Perfect.

1 They've had a long holiday last year.
2 She's travelled a lot in the past few years.
3 Have you lived in Madrid in 2005?
4 Did you get my message on Friday?
5 I've seen him several times recently.
6 He's started a new job a month ago.
7 I've phoned you three times yesterday.

2 Complete the sentences about *The North Face*. Use the correct form of the verb in brackets, Past Simple or Present Perfect.

1 In recent years *The North Face* _____ problems with people making illegal copies of its products. (have)

2 *The North Face* _____ eleven stores in Europe since 2003. (open)

3 In 2005 *The North Face* _____ its store in Livorno, Italy. (expand)

4 *The North Face* _____ a successful expedition to the mountain K2 in 1990. (sponsor)

5 *The North Face* _____ its products in serious sports magazines for many years. (advertise)

6 Ten years ago *The North Face* _____ TekWare, a new range of sportswear. (launch)

3 Complete the irregular verb table.

Infinitive	Past Simple	Past Participle
break	broke	broken
		flown
		forgotten
		had
		lost
		won

Pocket Book p.20

4 Work in pairs. Ask and answer questions. Write your partner's answers.

Example Student A *Have you ever flown in a helicopter?*
Student B *Yes, I have./No, I haven't.*

Have you ever …   My partner's answers
1 be/on television?
2 lose/something important?
3 break/an arm or leg?
4 win/a competition?
5 visit/another continent?
6 climb/a mountain?
7 forget/to do something important?
8 have/a holiday of more than
   three weeks?

5 Look at your partner's 'Yes' answers in **4**. Ask questions to get more information. Use the Past Simple.

Examples *When did you fly in a helicopter?*
Where did you fly to?
Did you enjoy it?

6 Tell the class three things about your partner.

UNIT 10 89

Wordpower

Verbs with prepositions

1 Work in pairs. Match words from A and B to describe the activities in the pictures. Then write the activity next to the picture.

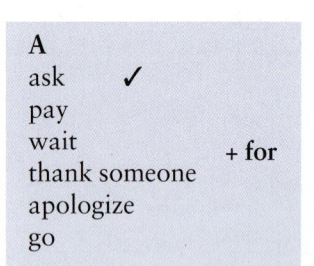

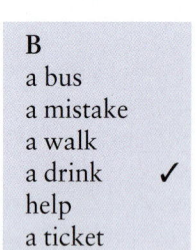

A	B
ask ✓	a bus
pay	a mistake
wait	a walk
thank someone + for	a drink ✓
apologize	help
go	a ticket

1. ask for a drink  
2. apologize for a mistake
3. 
4.
5.
6. 
7. 
8. 
9. 
10.

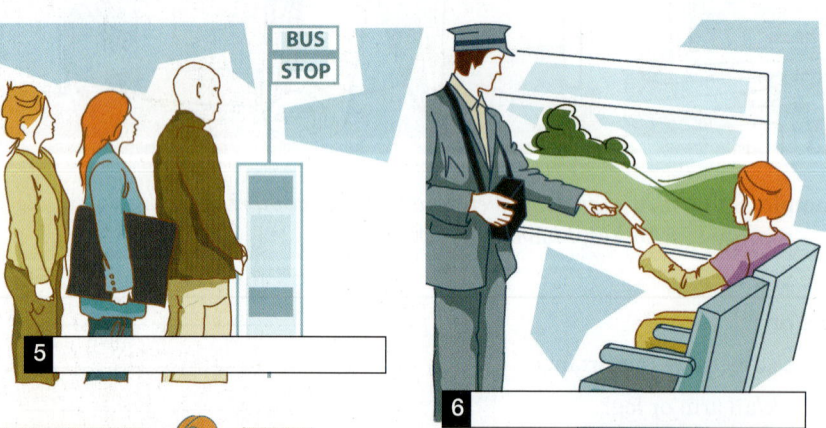

A	B
turn	holiday
put	a train
go + on	a TV
get	a jacket

90 UNIT 10

2 Complete the conversations with the words in the box.

| at | for | after | up |

1 Tom My daughter's sick. I have to stay at home to look _____ her. She's only three.
  Judith Fine. No problem.
2 Lara What's Harry's phone number?
  Frank I don't know. I'll look it _____ in the phone book.
3 Paul I've lost an important piece of paper.
  Sue Don't panic. I'll help you look _____ it.
4 Diane Have you looked _____ the photos I sent you yet?
  Katie Yes. I have. They are perfect for the company magazine.

3 🎧 10.6 Listen and check your answers to **2**.

4 Work in pairs. Look at the picture for one minute. Then close your books. Try to remember everything in the picture and describe what is happening. Use as many of the verbs with prepositions as you can.

Example *A woman is paying for a train ticket.*

Focus on communication

Answerphone messages

1 🎧 10.7 Listen to five answerphone messages. The sentences express the main idea of the message. Write the number of the call next to the message.

a Please dial a different number. ☐
b All the telephone lines are busy. ☐ *1*
c Please call when the office is open. ☐
d Please leave your name, address and postcode. ☐
e Please leave your name and telephone number. ☐

2 🎧 10.7 Listen again and complete the answerphone messages.

CALL 1 Thank you for _____ Airline Network. All our agents are _____ at the moment. Please _____ and an agent _____ your call as soon as possible.

CALL 2 The office is closed now. We are open from _____ to _____ Monday to Saturday. Please _____ during these times. In an emergency, please call 0118 956_____ .

CALL 3 The number you are dialling _____ . Please dial again , putting _____ before the last _____ digits.

CALL 4 This is Bob Steele's office. I'm sorry I can't take _____ right now but please leave your _____ and _____ and I'll _____ to you as soon as possible.

CALL 5 This is the Office World catalogue line. To _____ our catalogue , please leave your name, _____ and postcode, spelling any difficult _____ . Thank you for _____ .

3 🎧 10.7 Listen again and check your answers.

Emails and mobile phones

1 Read the email. What are the main differences between emails and letters?

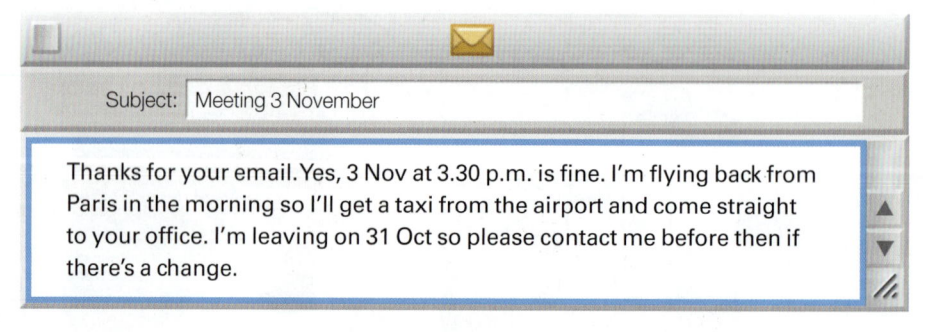

Subject: Meeting 3 November

Thanks for your email. Yes, 3 Nov at 3.30 p.m. is fine. I'm flying back from Paris in the morning so I'll get a taxi from the airport and come straight to your office. I'm leaving on 31 Oct so please contact me before then if there's a change.

2 🎧 10.8 Listen to a telephone conversation. Answer the questions.
1 Who is calling and why?
2 Where is she?
3 What problem does she have with her mobile phone?

3 Read the email. What makes it more personal than the email in **1** ?

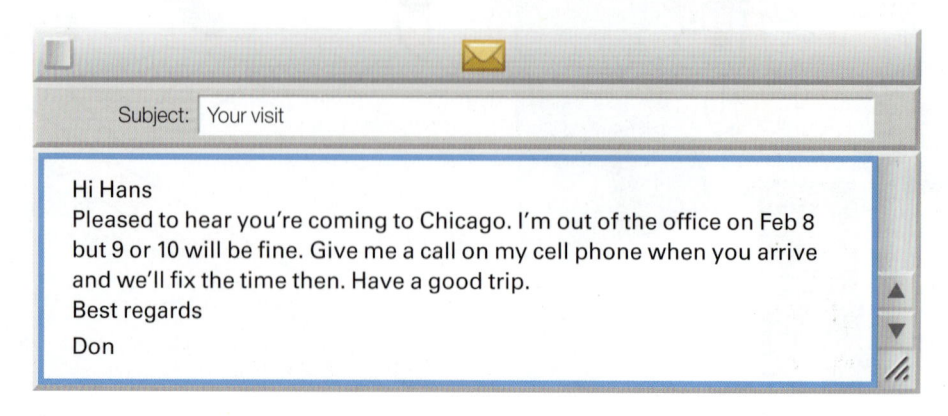

Subject: Your visit

Hi Hans
Pleased to hear you're coming to Chicago. I'm out of the office on Feb 8 but 9 or 10 will be fine. Give me a call on my cell phone when you arrive and we'll fix the time then. Have a good trip.
Best regards
Don

4 🎧 **10.9** Listen to the telephone conversation. Answer the questions.

1 Who are the speakers?
2 Are the speakers on mobile phones? How do you know?

5 🎧 **10.9** Listen again. Complete the conversation.

H Hello, Don, it's Hans. Am I disturbing you?
D Er … I'm in a restaurant with a customer at the moment, but we're getting ready to leave. _____¹ in about five minutes?
H Yes, of course.
   (Later)
H Don, Hans again. _____²?
D Yeah, _____³ before. So you've arrived?
H At last! It's a long trip. Oh, Don, _____⁴ … _____⁵ Don, the taxi driver wanted to check the address. Right, can we fix a time to meet?
D Sure. Tomorrow's best for me. _____⁶ to my office around twelve, then we have lunch together after?
H Good idea. _____⁷ tomorrow then.
D Yeah. Enjoy your first day in Chicago, Hans. Bye.

6 Work in pairs. Which of the telephone phrases below do you say

a at the beginning of the conversation?
b when you can't hear the person you're calling?

1 Am I disturbing you?
2 Sorry, we lost the connection.
3 Am I interrupting anything?
4 I can't hear you. Can you hang up and I'll call you again?
5 Is this a good time to call?
6 The line's breaking up. I'll call you again.
7 I think my mobile needs recharging.

7 Work in pairs. Prepare what to say in these mobile phone conversations. Then role-play the conversations.

STUDENT A

Conversation 1
You are staying in Milan. You are there for a furniture fair. Telephone a business contact to find out if he/she is going to the same fair. (You lose the connection at the beginning of the conversation so you have to call again.)

STUDENT B

Conversation 1
You are at a furniture fair in Milan. A business contact calls you on your mobile phone. You are discussing an order with a customer and don't want to talk to him/her now.

STUDENT B

Conversation 2
Call a friend of yours who is at the furniture fair. Ask if he/she would like to join you for dinner this evening.

STUDENT A

Conversation 2
You are at the furniture fair. A friend calls you on your mobile. You have invited an important customer to dinner at a restaurant this evening. (You can't hear. Ask your friend to hang up and call you again.)

📕 Pocket Book p.18

UNIT 10 93

REVIEW UNIT E

▼ AGENDA
▶ Grammar ❶ – ❸
▶ Vocabulary ❹, ❺
▶ Communication ❻, ❼

This unit reviews the main language points from Units 9 and 10. Complete the exercises. Check your learning with the self-check box at the end.

❶ Modal verbs
Complete the sentences with *should/shouldn't*, *have to/don't have to*, *can/can't*.

1 You ——— show your passport at the airport (it's necessary).
2 You ——— get a visa (it's not necessary).
3 You ——— check in ninety minutes before the flight (it's a good idea).
4 You ——— take one piece of hand luggage onto the plane (it's possible).
5 During the flight you ——— drink alcohol (it's not a good idea).
6 During the flight you ——— use your mobile phone (it's not possible).

❷ Present Perfect with *ever* and Past Simple
Write three questions for each conversation.

Example try skydiving
Have you ever tried skydiving?   Yes, I have.
When *did you try it?*   Last summer.
Where *did you try it?*   In Austria.

1 live in another country
A ——— ?
B Yes, I have.
A Where ——— ?
B In the USA.
A When ——— ?
B In 1999.

2 break a bone
A ——— ?
B Yes, I have.
A What ——— ?
B My right leg.
A How ——— ?
B I fell off my motorbike.

3 win a prize
A ——— ?
B Yes, I have.
A What ——— ?
B A holiday in California.
A When ——— ?
B Last year.

❸ Past Simple and Present Perfect
Underline the correct form of the verb, Past Simple or Present Perfect.

1 I *spent/have spent* six months in Africa in 1996.
2 Which places *did you visit/have you visited* on your last trip?
3 She *travelled/has travelled* a lot in the last month.
4 How many countries *did you travel/have you travelled* to recently?
5 *Did they arrive/Have they arrived* early yesterday evening?
6 The number of tourists *increased/has increased* a lot in recent years.
7 Last year all the hotels *were/have been* full.
8 This year four new hotels *opened/have opened*.

❹ Vocabulary: prepositions
Write the correct preposition: *for*, *on*, *to* or *up*.

1 Have you paid ——— the drinks?
2 Shall I turn ——— the TV?
3 I looked ——— the word in the dictionary.
4 Can you switch ——— the light? It's getting dark.
5 I can't find my passport. I've looked ——— it everywhere.
6 Will you wait ——— me? I won't be long.
7 It's very cold. Don't forget to put ——— warm clothes.
8 He apologized ——— the mistake he made.

94 ● REVIEW UNIT E

5 Vocabulary: hotel file

Complete the word.

1 You put your clothes in a s _ _ _ _ _ _ _ _ when you go on holiday.
2 You walk up s _ _ _ _ _ to get to the next floors in a building.
3 A l _ _ _ (BrE) or an e _ _ _ _ _ _ _ _ (AmE) takes you up to the next floors in a building.
4 You use s _ _ _ to wash with in the bathroom.
5 You use a t _ _ _ _ to dry yourself after a bath or shower.
6 You have to pay your hotel b _ _ _ when you check out of a hotel.
7 A r _ _ _ _ _ _ shows you have paid.
8 You need a k _ _ or a k _ _ _ _ _ _ to get into your hotel bedroom.

6 Invitations and suggestions

Complete the conversations. Use different phrases for each gap.

1 A Ms Davido, ――――――――――― see our new conference centre?
   B Thank you. That ―――――――――― .

2 A Jack. ――――――――――― playing golf on Saturday?
   B I'd ――――――――――― , but unfortunately I have to leave on Saturday morning.

3 A José, ――――――――――― have dinner with us this evening?
   B Thanks very much. I'd ――――――――――― .

4 A Hi, Giulia. Are you busy this evening?
   B No, why?
   A ――――――――――― coming with us for a pizza after the lesson?
   B Yes, ――――――――――― .

5 A Jason, why ――――――――――― go sailing next weekend?
   B I'm ――――――――――― , but I have to study. I've got an exam on Monday.

6 A Are you doing anything on Friday evening, Alex?
   B No, I don't think so.
   A Then ――――――――――― go out for a meal?
   B That's ――――――――――― .

7 Telephoning: mobile phones

Work in pairs. What do you say when you call a person on their mobile phone

1 again, because you lost the connection?
2 to check you're not phoning at a bad time?
3 and the line becomes very weak?
4 and the battery in your mobile phone is low?

Look at the self-check box. Tick the areas you need to review again.

SELF-CHECK BOX	Yes	No	Pocket Book
• Modal verbs			6
• Past Simple and Present Perfect			8, 10
• Vocabulary: prepositions			24
• Vocabulary: hotel file			
• Invitations and suggestions			15, 16
• Telephoning: mobile phones			18

REVIEW UNIT E

Listening scripts

Unit 1
1.1
I=Interviewer, SD=Stephanie Debord
I   Stephanie Debord, could you tell us something about yourself?
SD Yes, of course.
I   Thank you. First, where are you from?
SD I'm from Belgium.
I   Where do you live?
SD I live in Laforêt in the south of Belgium.
I   Do you work in Laforêt?
SD Yes, I do.
I   What do you do?
SD I'm a lawyer.
I   Which company do you work for?
SD Legal Laforêt.
I   Do you enjoy your job?
SD Yes, I do.
I   Are you single?
SD No, I'm married.
I   Is your husband a lawyer too?
SD No, he's a teacher.
I   Do you have any children?
SD Yes, we have two daughters, Emilie and Lara.
I   How old are they?
SD They're three.
I   They're twins!
SD Yes, that's right.

1.2
I=Interviewer, SD=Stephanie Debord
I   Stephanie, can you tell us about a typical working day? What time do you get up?
SD I get up at seven fifteen. I have breakfast with my children and I get them ready for playschool.
I   What time do you leave home?
SD I leave home at eight.
I   How do you go to work?
SD I take the children to playschool, then I go to work by bike.
I   And what time do you get to work?
SD Oh, uhm, at about eight forty.
I   Uhm, so what time do you finish work?
SD I finish at three.
I   Three! That's early. So … do you get home at three forty?
SD No, I don't. I go to the playschool and pick up my girls. We get home at er… four.

1.3
1   Are you Spanish?
2   Is he a lawyer?
3   Do you come from Italy?
4   Do you work in Rome?
5   Do you have any children?
6   Where do you live?
7   What do you do?
8   Where do you work?
9   How do you go to work?
10 What time do you get home?

1.4
Conversation 1
I=Interviewer, S=Stephanie Debord
I   Stephanie, can you describe some of the things you do every day at work?
S   Oh! I read my emails, then write replies. I do all my email in the morning.
I   Mmm-hmm.
S   I'm a lawyer so I read a lot at work: emails, documents, information.
I   Right.
S   But I work with people a lot too. I make a lot of phone calls. I talk for … er… maybe four hours a day on the phone.
I   That's a lot!
S   But I also have meetings with clients and I give them advice. Sometimes we have a meeting all day and then I have lunch with the clients.
I   Do you have meetings with colleagues too?
S   Yes. I have a lot of meetings with colleagues. Uhm, because, we work together on projects.
I   And do you travel to other cities or countries?
S   No. All our clients are here in Laforêt.

Conversation 2
I=Interviewer, T=Timo Kekkonen
I   Timo, good morning.
T   Morning.
I   Er … Timo, what do you do on a typical working day?
T   A typical day? Hmm. I read the financial newspapers. I read them for about an hour. I also read the news on the Internet.
I   Yes.
T   Yes. Then I read and reply to my emails. We work with clients in the USA and they send emails at night. Er … because of the time difference.
I   Do you talk on the telephone a lot?
T   Yes, I do because my clients are in different countries.
I   So, do you travel to other cities and countries?
T   Yes, I do. To Sweden, the USA. I have meetings with clients and we have lunch together.
I   Do you meet your colleagues in the USA?
T   Yes, when I go to New York. Two times a year, I have meetings with my US colleagues.

1.5
M=Menno, A=Alice, W=William, E=Evelyn
A   Hello, I'm Alice. Your new teacher.
M   Nice to meet you. I'm Menno. This way please. The class is in my office. Is that OK?
A   Fine. I often teach in offices. It's no problem.
M   Excellent.
W   Nice to meet you. I'm William.
A   Nice to meet you, William.
E   I'm Evelyn.
A   Pleased to meet you Evelyn. Do you know William and Menno?
E   No. I work in a different department.
M   I'm Menno. I work in Accounts.
W   William. I work in Marketing. Where do you work Evelyn?
E   I work in Reception. I'm a receptionist.
A   OK. Let's start the lesson.

1.6
M=Menno, A=Alice, E=Evelyn, W=William
A   Menno, do you have a whiteboard?
M   Oh, I'm sorry, no. I don't need a whiteboard in my job.
A   Oh. Uhm … OK I can write the notes on a piece of paper.
E   No, no, we have a whiteboard in the other office. In Dirk's office. We can use that.
A   Great!
…
A   Now we have a listening lesson. Uhm … where is the CD player?
M   Sorry, Alice, I don't have a CD player.
A   Oh no!
W   It's OK. I have my laptop. We can play the CD on my computer.
A   Good idea! Thank you, William.
W   No problem.

1.7
Conversation 1
A   Dieter, can I introduce you to José Corra? José, this is Dieter Hann.
B   Pleased to meet you.
C   Pleased to meet you, too.
A   José is the manager at our office in Barcelona.

Conversation 2
A   Can I introduce myself? My name is Pietro Zenari.
B   Hello. Nice to meet you. I'm Jackie Pons.

Conversation 3
A   Lisa, do you know Marcel Tullier? Marcel, this is a colleague of mine, Lisa White.
B   Hello, Lisa. Nice to meet you.
C   Hi, nice to meet you too, Marcel.

1.8
Conversation 1
A   Hello, Franca. How are you?
B   Very well, thanks, Brad. And you?
A   Fine, thanks. How's the family?
B   Very well, thanks.

Conversation 2
A   Bye, Marco. Thanks for everything.
B   It was great seeing you, John.
A   See you again soon.
B   Yes, bye.

Conversation 3
A   Good morning, Monsieur Gilot. It's good to see you again.
B   Good morning, Elena. It's nice to be here again.
A   How's everything in Paris?
B   Fine, thanks. Very busy as always.

Conversation 4
A   Well, goodbye, Mr Ross. It was nice meeting you.
B   I enjoyed meeting you, too. Have a good trip.
A   Thank you. I hope to see you again soon. Goodbye.
B   Goodbye, Mr Adaz.

Unit 2

2.1

/s/	/z/	/ɪz/
starts	lives	finishes
works	does	discusses
gets	arrives	watches
speaks	travels	studies
makes	leaves	

2.2

Stephanie
Er … in the evening I always read the newspaper. I never watch TV in the evening because my daughters always want to watch cartoons. At the weekend I often go shopping in the supermarket. I invite friends to my house and we have parties … parties with adults and children. All my friends have children. I sometimes go cycling at the weekend. If the weather's nice …

Timo
I work very late so I always relax when I get home. I watch TV. I usually play my guitar three or four times a week, with my friends. At the weekend I go swimming. In winter I sometimes go skiing. I love sport but er… I hardly ever go the gym. I don't have time!

2.3

Jörgen
What kind of holidays do I enjoy? Well, I really enjoy travelling to new places. I like lots of activity when I'm on holiday. I love walking and trekking – my next holiday is trekking in the jungle in Thailand. I don't enjoy doing nothing when I'm on holiday. For example, I don't like lying on a beach. OK, sometimes, when I'm very tired, I can relax on a beach for two days, but then I'm ready for something active again!

2.4

a thirteen
b thirty

2.5

1 14
2 60
3 70
4 18

2.6

1 43
2 24
3 16
4 55
5 97
6 72

2.7

1 It's seven o'clock.
2 It's eleven twenty.
3 It's three oh five.
4 It's eight forty.
5 It's nine forty-five.

2.8

A Good morning. L. S. Communications. How can I help you?
B Good morning. Can I speak to Anna Pilon, please?
A Just a moment, please.
C Hello.
B Hello. Is that Anna Pilon?
C Yes, speaking.
B This is Mario Bardo. I'm calling about …

2.9

R=Receptionist, P=Pete May, J=Jon Dunn
R AMC Design. How can I help you?
P Oh, hello. Could I speak to Jon Dunn, please?
R Who's calling, please?
P It's Pete May from Novac.
R Hold on, please.
J Hello, Pete. It's Jon. How are you?
P Fine, thanks, Jon. I'm phoning about our next meeting. Are you free on Thursday afternoon, at 4 o'clock?

Unit 3

3.1

R=Rachel, C=Chris
R Hi Chris! How's your first day?
C Hello Rachel. Everything is fine. I'm so happy! I have my own office – great!
R Yes! This is a great place to work, Chris. So, have you got everything you need?
C OK … I have a computer and a keyboard, but the computer doesn't have a mouse.
R Yes, it does. The mouse is in the green box.
C Oh … yes. Oops. I don't have a printer.
R No, there's only one printer in the office. It's in Yuri's room.
C OK. Uhm …
R Have you got a phone?
C No. I haven't.
R OK. Don't worry. I can get one for you.
C Thanks.
R Have you got pens and paper?
C Yes. I have.
R Do you have a diary?
C No, I don't.
R There are some diaries in my office. Come and see me in a minute. Do you need a calendar too?
C No, it's OK. I've got a calendar. Er.. it's here.
R And you need some pictures on the walls.
C Yes. Where do I get them?
R The shops! You have to buy the pictures yourself!
C Oh!

3.2

R=Rachel, C=Chris
R Ah Chris, here's your diary.
C Thanks Rachel. So, where do people eat lunch?
R Most people eat a sandwich or go out for lunch. There isn't a canteen in the office.
C Right. And drinks? Is there a coffee machine in the office?
R No, there isn't. There is a little kitchen downstairs and the coffee machine is in the kitchen.
C Ah. And my office is a bit hot today. Has the office got air conditioning?
R No. We haven't got air conditioning in the office.
C Oh no.
R There is air-con in one room, in Yuri's room, for the computers. But not in the other offices.
C OK. Er … I want to drive to work. Are there any parking spaces?
R Sorry. No, there aren't. There's a car park in the next street.
C Oh.
R There is one parking space in the office.
C Is there?
R For the manager!
C Oh.

3.3

1 There's only one printer in the office.
2 There are some chairs and magazines in reception.
3 There aren't any books in her office.
4 Are there any parking spaces?
5 I've got a calendar.
6 Has the office got air conditioning?

3.4

K=Katrin, J=Julia, S=Sara, B=Boris, D=Diana, V=Vincent

Conversation 1
K Julia?
J Hi Katrin. Where are you?
K I'm on the corner of Museum Road and the High Street. There's a theatre opposite.
J Right. I'm uhm … I'm near the café, on the left of the tables outside.
K Oh, OK. Just a minute. Yes, I can see you!

Conversation 2
S Boris! Where are you?
B I'm at the bus stop in front of a hotel called 'The Sands'.
S Oh. Is that the one on the seafront?
B Yes, that's right.
S I'm on the same road, just in front of the conference centre, the other side of Museum Road.
B OK. I can see you.

Conversation 3
D Vincent, it's Diana. I'm on the High Street, on the right of the big steps outside the museum.
V Ah, right. I'm in a restaurant. It's near the seafront.
D Is that the Chinese restaurant on the High Street?
V No, it's next to the bookshop on Seafront Road.
D OK. I'll come and find you.

3.5

Conversation 1
J=Julia, K=Katrin, P=Passer-by 1
J We need to check in first. Any idea where the hotel is?
K No, let's ask. Excuse me, where is the Sanders Hotel?
P1 Ah, yes. Let me think. It's on the High Street. On the corner of Hill Street, opposite the Chinese restaurant.
J Thank you.

Conversation 2
B=Boris, S=Sara, P2=Passer-by 2, P3=Passer-by 3
B Hi Sara.
S Boris!
B We need to get a taxi. Any ideas?
S I think there's a taxi rank by the seafront.
B Oh, sorry … Excuse me, is there a taxi rank near here?
P2 I'm sorry, I don't know.
B OK. Thanks. Excuse me, is there a taxi rank near here?
P3 Uhm, it's on Seafront Road, in front of the conference centre.
B Thanks very much.

Conversation 3
D=Diana, V=Vincent, P4=Passer-by 4
D I'm really hungry.
V Me too. Gerhardt is having lunch in an Italian restaurant.
D Gerhardt - the sales manager for Germany?
V Yes. I think he said it's on Museum Road.
D I'll ask. Excuse me, we're looking for an Italian restaurant.
P4 An Italian Restaurant?
V It's called something *Mare*.
P4 Oh yes, *Il Mare*. It's on the High Street just next to the department store.
D Great. Thanks.

3.6

V=Visitor, M=Man, W=Woman

Conversation 1
V Excuse me, I'm looking for the shopping centre.
M Cross over the road and walk down Princes Street. Turn first left at the crossroads, then turn second right. The shopping centre is about 50 metres along that road on the right.
V So, down Princes Street, left at the crossroads and then second right?
M Yes, that's right.
V Thanks a lot.

LISTENING SCRIPTS 97

Conversation 2
V   Excuse me, is the museum near here?
W   Let's see ... yes. Go right down here. At the traffic lights turn left and go straight on to the square. The museum is in the square, on the right.
V   Sorry, could you say that again?
W   Yes. Go right down here. At the traffic lights turn left. Then go straight on to the square. The museum is in the square, on the right.
V   Thank you very much.

Conversation 3
V   Excuse me, is the sports centre straight on?
M   No, the sports centre is left down here. Go along this road. There's a bridge on the left. Go over the bridge, then turn first right, then first left. The sports centre is at the end of the road, on the left, after the cinema.
V   Many thanks.

3.7
P=Passenger, C=Ticket office clerk
P   Hello, a single ticket to Victoria, please.
C   Single to Victoria? That's £17.50.
P   Sorry, could you repeat that?
C   Yes, £17.50.
P   Can I have a receipt, please?
C   Sure. Here you are.
P   Thank you. What time's the next train?
C   At five thirty. In eleven minutes.
P   Which platform does it leave from?
C   Platform two, over the bridge.
P   How long does the journey take?
C   Forty-five minutes.
P   Thanks very much for your help.
C   Not at all.

Unit 4
4.1

/d/	/t/	/ɪd/
borrowed	asked	decided
followed	finished	invited
lived	liked	wanted
showed	worked	
travelled		

4.2
J=Journalist, TW=Tony Wheeler
J   First, Tony, why did you go to Australia?
TW Well, at that time Maureen and I wanted to make a long journey before we returned to live and work in London. So we decided to go to Australia, and travel through Europe, the Middle East, and Asia.
J   Did you return to London after that long journey?
TW No, we didn't. We decided we really liked travelling so we travelled again and wrote another book.
J   Did you write your first book in Sydney?
TW Yes, we did. We had a very small flat in Sydney and we wrote the book on our kitchen table!
J   How much money did you take?
TW You mean on our journey to Australia?
J   Yes.
TW We took $1,200 and of course we spent it all. When we arrived in Sydney we had only 27 cents.
J   So not much left! How did you sell the book?
TW Well, I went to all the bookshops in Sydney and showed them the book. In one bookshop the buyer was very interested and he showed it to his girlfriend. That was very lucky because his girlfriend was a journalist for the *Sydney Morning Herald* and she asked me …

4.3
L=Laura, M=Mohammed
L   Oh, Mohammed, China! Where did you go? Beijing? Shanghai?
M   No, I went to Guangzhou and Hong Kong. In the south of China. I went to our new factories there.
L   Hong Kong too! Great. When did you go?
M   I went last month.
L   How long did you stay there?
M   Nine days. One week in Guangzhou and a weekend in Hong Kong.
L   How did you travel?
M   In Guangzhou we went by car and we went to Hong Kong by ferry.
L   Interesting. What was the weather like?
M   It was wet, rainy, and cold! The weather was awful.
L   Oh no! Uhm.. so, who did you go with?
M   I went with our regional manager, David Wong.
L   Oh I know David. He's really nice.
M   Yeah, he was great.
L   And … er, where did you stay?
M   We stayed in five-star hotels all the time. David found the hotels and they were fabulous!
L   So, did you have a good time?
M   Yeah, I loved it. It was hard work but it was great.

4.4
A=Switchboard operator, B=Ron Basca
A   Good morning. Sava Electronics.
B   Good morning. Can I have extension 473, please?
A   One moment please. I'm sorry, the line's busy. Will you hold?
B   Er, no, I'll call again later. Thank you. Goodbye.
A   Goodbye.

4.5
A=Switchboard operator, B = Ron Basca, C=Personal Assistant
A   Good morning. Sava Electronics.
B   Good morning. Can I have extension 473, please?
A   Yes. One moment, please.
B   Hello. Is that Carla Mann?
C   No, it's her PA. I'm sorry, but she's in a meeting. Can I take a message?
B   Yes, please. Could you ask her to call me? My name's Ron Basca and the number is 01483 675 9982.
C   Sorry, could you say that again?
B   Yes, 01483 675 9982.
C   Thank you. Could you spell your name, please?
B   Yes. Ron, that's R-O-N, Basca, B-A-S-C-A.
C   Thank you, Mr Basca. I'll give her your message.
B   Thanks a lot. Goodbye.

4.6
1 Can I have extension 473, please?
2 I'm sorry, but she's in a meeting.
3 Can I take a message?
4 Could you ask her to call me?
5 Sorry, could you say that again?
6 Could you spell your name, please?
7 I'll give her your message.

4.7
a 0208-553-9057
b 0143-4285611
c 75-30-6929
d 001212-5315898

4.8

(say)	(he)	(egg)	(eye)	(go)	(bar)	(you)
/eɪ/	/iː/	/e/	/aɪ/	/əʊ/	/ɑː/	/uː/
a	b	f	i	o	r	q
h	c	l	y			u
j	d	m				w
k	e	n				
	g	s				
	p	x				
	t	*z (BrE)				
	v					
	*z (AmE)					

4.9
1 French   4 Spanish
2 Italian   5 Thai
3 Polish   6 Brazilian

Unit 5
5.1
J=Journalist, O=World Tourism Organization official
J   Now, you say there was a very big increase in tourism in the 1960s. I'd like some information about that. Can you give me some figures, starting before 1960? How many tourists were there in 1950?
O   Well, there weren't many international tourists then, only 25 million, but 20 years later, in 1970, the number increased to 166 million, so for that period, it was a very big change.
J   Yes, from 25 million to 166 million in 20 years.
O   Yes, and this increase continued. In 1990 there were 458 million and in 2000, 698 million.
J   So in just ten years the number went up from 458 million to 698?
O   That's right. It was a very big increase.
J   And how about the future?
O   The situation may change. For example, oil prices may go up. But the prediction now is that there will be over one and a half billion tourists by 2020.

5.2
J=Journalist, TE= Tourism expert
J   Nowadays ecotourism is very popular. Can you tell us about it?
TE Of course. Ecotourism really began in the 1990s and it's now very popular. The industry grew about 20% last year. That's three times faster than general tourism.
J   Wow. Which countries are popular at the moment?
TE There are a lot of popular countries: South Africa and Mexico, for example. Costa Rica is very popular. It has amazing jungles and a beautiful coast.
J   And how much money does an average visitor spend?
TE A visitor to Costa Rica spends about $1,000. That's good business: $1,000 is a lot of money in Costa Rica. Visitors to France only spend an average of $400.
J   And where do ecotourists stay?
TE Well, there isn't much demand for big hotel resorts.
J   Why?
TE Hotels use too many resources – electricity, gas, and so on. Most ecotourists stay in lodges. These lodges don't use many resources and they employ local people.
J   Does ecotourism make much money for Costa Ricans?
TE Yes. Ecotourism brings a lot of money into the country. This makes an income of around $140 per person each year. The total income for Costa Rica last year was $1.34 billion.

5.3

A	B	C
apples	broccoli	bananas
carrots	oranges	potatoes
chicken	strawberries	tomatoes
chocolate		
mushrooms		
onions		
yogurt		

5.4
P=Pete, J=Jon
P   Welcome to Novac, Jon.
J   Hi, Pete. Good to see you again. How's everything?
P   Oh, fine, thanks. What about you?
J   Very busy right now. A lot of travelling.
P   Yes. I can see that. Can I take your coat?
J   Thanks.
P   Would you like something to drink? A coffee, a cold drink?
J   Yeah, I'd like a coffee, please.
P   … Oh, Elena, er, can you bring us two coffees, please?

Thanks … Well, Jon, we've got a lot to do today. Shall I begin with the programme?
J Yes, OK. Oh, could you give me a couple of minutes, I need to make a call.
P Of course. Go ahead.

5.5
1 Can I take your coat?
2 Would you like something to drink?
3 Can you bring us two coffees, please?
4 Shall I begin with the programme?
5 Could you give me a couple of minutes?

5.6
W=Waitress, P=Pete, J=Jon
P Right, Jon. We have about an hour for lunch. The next meeting is at two thirty.
J That's good. I usually only have time for a quick sandwich for lunch, often at my desk!
W Are you ready to order?
P Er, yes, I think so. What would you like, Jon?
J I'll have the salmon pâté with toast, and the omelette.
W Right.
P And I'd like the soup and the chicken casserole.
W So that's one salmon pâté and soup, then one omelette, and one chicken casserole. Would you like vegetables or a side salad?
P Jon?
J I'll have a side salad, please.
P And I'd like vegetables.
W Right. And would you like something to drink?
J Yes, a glass of white wine.
P I'll have a beer, please. Could you bring us some mineral water too?
W Certainly. Would you like still or sparkling?
P Jon?
J Still, please.
W Right.
P Thank you.

Unit 6
6.1
I=Interviewer, M=Martina
I Martina, were you on the train all the time?
M No. If you want, you can can go on excursions and do activities. I got off the train at the Blue Mountains.
I The Blue Mountains. It sounds lovely!
M But I was there at the weekend when they are busier and more crowded.
I Crowded?
M People from the cities go there because of the cleaner air and the scenery.
I But there are a lot of people?
M Yes. And it was summer so everything was more expensive.
I Oh no!
M It was OK because I went mountain biking with a friend and we found some quieter places. We didn't cycle a long way because my friend was older than me. After an hour cycling he was tired.
I What else can people do?
M Well, I saw people rock climbing, … abseiling.
I Did you go rock climbing?
M No! The rock climbers were younger and … more adventurous tourists than me! I was happy cycling.

6.2
I=Interviewer, TC=Travel consultant
I So, this survey compares the cost of a short holiday in major cities. Which city is the most expensive for a tourist to visit?
TC There's no change from the last survey. It's London.
I Of course.
TC London was the most expensive at $900. That's almost twice the average of $470!
I I'm not surprised. Everything is expensive there: taxis, hotels, eating out … But the museums are often free.
TC True. But $900 is a lot of money.
I And what about Paris? Tokyo? New York?
TC Tokyo is more expensive than New York. But, er…Paris is cheaper than Tokyo. In fact, yes, Paris and New York were the same … $670.
I My last weekend break was in Madrid. Where is it in the survey?
TC It's cheaper than Paris and New York. Er … Madrid was $550.
I Right. And which cities were cheapest for a short stay?
TC Well, cities outside of Europe. Prices were lower in Bangkok and São Paulo. In São Paulo the price is $290 and in Bangkok just a little higher at $340.
I Bangkok $340 and São Paulo $290?
TC Yes. But the lowest for a short stay is in Europe, in Prague.
I And what's the cost there?
TC Prague is … $270.
I $270! Wow. So you can go to Prague three times for the cost of one stay in London!
TC That's right. Um, … There really are very big differences between major cities …

6.3
1 the first of May or May the first
2 the second of April or April the second
3 the tenth of March or March the tenth
4 the nineteenth of August or August the nineteenth
5 the twenty-fourth of September or September the twenty-fourth

6.4
1 the seventeenth
2 the thirtieth
3 the sixteenth
4 the twelfth

6.5
1 the third of April
2 the fourth of June
3 the twentieth of March
4 the twenty-third of September
5 the thirteenth of November
6 the thirtieth of December

6.6
The British English way
1 the first of February nineteen ninety-nine
2 the sixth of August two thousand
3 the eleventh of June two thousand and six
4 the seventh of May two thousand and seven
5 the third of April two thousand and one
6 the second of October two thousand and ten

The American English way
1 January second nineteen ninety-nine
2 June eighth two thousand
3 November sixth two thousand and six
4 July fifth two thousand and seven
5 March fourth two thousand and one
6 February tenth two thousand and ten

6.7
Conversation 1
P1=passenger 1, P2=Passenger 2
P1 What's wrong?
P2 How much is your train ticket?
P1 €1.10.
P2 That's the problem. You have a fifty-euro note. The machine doesn't accept big notes.
P1 Oh no!
P2 Do you have any coins?
P1 No. Only the note.
P2 Sorry. Then, you can't use the machine.
P1 Oh!

Conversation 2
C=Customer, W=Waiter
W How was your meal, sir?
C Delicious. Excellent. Mmm. Here's the bill and my card.
W Oh. Er… I'm sorry sir, we don't accept cards.
C No?
W No. We don't accept any cards.
C Oh no!
W Do you have cash?
C No.
W I'm very sorry sir, but we have to go together to a cash machine, to get the money.
C Oh.
W I'll get my coat.

Conversation 3
C=Customer, CCO=Call centre operator
CCO So your flight is booked from London to Istanbul.
C Excellent.
CCO The cost is €220.
C Can I pay by credit card?
CCO Yes. It's more expensive to pay by credit card. It's … an extra €5.
C Ah. Uhm, I also have my debit card. Maestro.
CCO A debit card doesn't cost any extra money.
C OK. I'll use my debit card.
CCO Can I have the number please?
C Yes. It's …

6.8
Conversation 1
A=Mr Alvarez, C=Mike Carr
C Mr Alvarez?
A Yes.
C How do you do? My name's Mike Carr.
A Pleased to meet you, Mr Carr.
C I hope you had a good flight.
A Yes. The plane left late but we arrived on time.
C That's good. My car is parked just outside.
A Thank you for meeting me.
C Not at all. Is this your first visit to Dublin?
A No, I was here last year. I really like it. What about you? Do you come from Dublin?
C No, but my parents came here when I was a child. And you, do you live in Barcelona?
A Yes, right in the centre.
C And where do you work?
A Just outside Barcelona. About fifteen kilometres to the north.
C And do you travel a lot for work?
A Not a lot. I make four or five business trips abroad every year, and we sometimes have a short break in a European city. We went to Prague for a few days last month.
C Really? I was in Prague last week. It's a beautiful city. We plan to do business with a company there … so I hope I can go there again soon …

LISTENING SCRIPTS 99

6.9
Conversation 2
A=Mr Abbott, P=Ms Peto
A Welcome to New York, Ms Peto. Did you have a good trip?
P Yes, it was fine, thanks. It's great to be here.
A Is it your first time in New York?
P Yes, it is. It's a very exciting city.
A It sure is. How long are you here for?
P Only four days. I leave on Friday.
A Oh, that's too bad. Do you travel abroad much?
P Yes, quite a lot. I was in London last week and next week I go to Germany.
A Do you enjoy travelling?
P Yes, I find it interesting. But on a business trip there isn't any time to see the places you want to see.
A No, that's true. Is everything at the hotel OK?
P Oh yes, the hotel's great, thanks.
A Good. Now, let me introduce you to some of my colleagues …

Unit 7

7.1
I=Interviewer, K=Kazuko
I Kazuko, you're Japanese but you live in America. Can you tell us why?
K Yes, of course. I'm a freelance journalist and I write about the USA, mainly about politics and business.
I I see. Do you write for newspapers … or magazines?
K Yes, for both. I write articles for two newspapers and a business magazine. They're all Japanese of course … and I also do work for TV companies, special reports for business programmes … that sort of thing.
I Sounds very interesting … and what are you …

7.2
I=Interviewer, K=Kazuko
I Kazuko, what are you working on currently?
K Well, this week I'm writing about the elections, here in the US. It's a lot of work! I'm interviewing politicians and talking to lots of people, getting information, that sort of thing …
I Are you travelling a lot, then?
K Yes, I am. Normally I drive everywhere but this week I'm not making any trips by car because I haven't got much time. I'm going everywhere by plane.
I Yeah.
K Oh, I'm also preparing a special report on the US computer industry.
I Are you interviewing people for that project?
K No, I'm not, fortunately! I can do all the work at home for this, with the help of my computer of course!
I Well you certainly have an interesting job, Kazuko. Thank you and good luck with both projects …
K Thanks.

7.3
1 He's working here.
2 You're winning the game.
3 We're going on holiday.
4 I'm listening to the radio.
5 She's helping them.
6 They're playing football.

7.4
1 He isn't working here.
2 You aren't winning the game.
3 We aren't going on holiday.
4 I'm not listening to the radio.
5 She isn't helping them.
6 They aren't playing football.

7.5
L=Lara, M=Max
M Hello.
L Hello, is that Max Cromer?
M Yes, speaking.
L Max, it's Lara. Do you remember the visitors from China I told you about? Well, they're arriving next Monday. Can we arrange a meeting?
M Yes, of course. How long are they staying?
L For a week. Is Tuesday possible for you?
M No, I'm sorry, I'm busy on Tuesday. I'm visiting customers all day. What about Wednesday?
L No, that isn't possible. They're going to a trade fair on Wednesday. How about Thursday?
M Thursday afternoon's OK.
L Good. What time? Two thirty at your office?
M Yes, that's fine. So, two thirty this Thursday, at my office?
L Yes. Thanks, Max. See you on Thursday, then.

7.6
M Hello, Max Cromer.
L Hello, Max. It's Lara. I'm very sorry but we've got a problem on Thursday. Can we change the date of our meeting?
M Yes, of course. When are you free?
L Well, any time on Friday or Monday afternoon is OK for us.
M Friday's not possible for me because I'm flying to Brussels for the day. What about Monday afternoon?
L That's fine. What time do you prefer?
M Is three fifteen OK?
L Yes, that's fine.
M Good. See you next Monday at three fifteen, then.
L Thanks a lot Max, and sorry again.
M That's no problem. Goodbye, Lara.

Unit 8

8.1
1
Here are the answers to the South Korea Quiz.
1 The population of Seoul, the capital of South Korea, is about 11,000,000. Answer a.
2 The South Korean currency is the won, spelt w-o-n. Answer c.
3 The average maximum temperature in Seoul in August is about 31 degrees centigrade. Answer b.
4 The second biggest city in South Korea is Busan. It's also known as Pusan, with a 'p'. Answer b.
5 Soju is an alcoholic drink made from rice. Answer c.

2
Now here are the answers to the Poland Quiz.
1 Seven. Poland has a border with seven countries. They are Russia, Lithuania, Belarus, Ukraine, Slovakia, the Czech Republic, and Germany. Answer c.
2 Poland joined the EU in May 2004. Answer c.
3 The average minimum temperature in Warsaw in January is minus six degrees centigrade. Answer a.
4 In Poland people traditionally eat fish for Christmas. Answer b.
5 The second biggest city in Poland is Łódź. Answer a.

8.2
E=*Europa magazine* journalist, LJ=Lee Jin
E Lee Jin, Karol Lazienki is moving to Korea for work.
LJ Uh-huh.
E What will his life be like?
LJ It will be great. He will love it. I'm sure he will love it.
E But he'll be a foreigner in a new country. I mean … will it be difficult to meet people?
LJ No! No, it won't. People in Korea are really friendly and lots of people will invite him out.
E What kind of places will he go out to?
LJ Well, after work, he will probably go out to bars, restaurants with his colleagues. People like to go out and they will invite Karol to come too.
E And what is the food like?
LJ Delicious. But er … it's also very spicy so maybe he will need to be a little careful.
E Spicy?
LJ It's hot! It has a lot of garlic, yes, a lot of chilli.
E What will his new office be like?
LJ It will probably be quite formal. The men will wear a suit and tie. That's normal in South Korea.
E OK.
LJ Another thing that is different is that people are very interested in you.
E Will they ask him personal questions?
LJ Yes, they will. And they will ask him personal questions everywhere: at work, in the office, everywhere.
E What kind of questions will the Koreans ask him?
LJ They will ask 'Are you married?' 'How much do you earn?' Yes.
E Really?
LJ Yeah. And why not? People want to know about you.

8.3
1 He'll come later.
2 You'll feel better soon.
3 She'll be here on Friday.
4 We'll get the news tomorrow.
5 It won't rain today.
6 You won't have any problems.
7 They won't be at the meeting.
8 I won't leave this evening.

8.4
KS=Kim Soo, KL=Karol Lazienki
KL Soo. Hello.
KS Hello Karol. I'm looking forward to coming to Poland next week. A week in Warsaw and two days in Łódź.
KL That's right! I'm sure it will be an interesting visit for you.
KS Er … I'm phoning because I have some questions.
KL OK.
KS What will the weather be like?
KL Ah … It's very cold at the moment and the weathermen say it'll snow next week.
KS Ah. I thought so.
KL And when it snows, the sun is very bright. So I think you'll need sunglasses too.
KS Right. There is one other thing I am worried about. Will people speak English?
KL Er … yes. I think so. Don't worry. You won't have any language problems.
KS Great. Er … Those are all my questions.
KL OK. Well, see you next week.

8.5
address c
envelope a
postcode/zip code d
stamp b
fax machine f
mobile/cellphone e
phone with answerphone g
attachment i
CD-ROM r
desktop PC m
disk drive n
email address h
keyboard l
laptop j
monitor k
mouse p
USB port o
printer q

8.6
1 The website is www dot freeserve dot net. That's freeserve, all one word, dot n-e-t.
2 My email address is j underscore ellis. That's e double-l i-s at dialstart, that's d-i-a-l-s-t-a-r-t dot co dot uk.
3 My email address is timflan. That's all one word, t-i-m-f-l-a-n at a-o-l dot com.

8.7
1 The website is www.cnn.com.
2 The website is www.healthnet.org.uk. That's h-e-a-l-t-h-n-e-t dot o-r-g dot uk.
3 My email address is russelg@clara.net. That's russel, r-u-s-s-e-l, g, at clara, that's c-l-a-r-a dot net.
4 My email address is p.pezzini@rol.com. That's p dot pezzini. That's p-e-z-z-i-n-i at r-o-l dot com.
5 My email address is roychapman@altavista.net. r-o-y-c-h-a-p-m-a-n all one word and altavista is a-l-t-a-v-i-s-t-a.

Unit 9
9.1
a You can stay in a private room.
b You can't make a prison into a hotel!

9.2
1 You can stay in a converted prison.
2 You can't go by car.
3 Can we ski?
4 Yes, you can.
5 You can't invite a lot of guests.
6 You can't take risks.
7 Can you park your car in the hotel?
8 No, you can't.

9.3
Reception	Bedroom	Bathroom
lift or elevator f	blanket k	bath u
stairs d	hangers m	shower q
luggage a	pillow j	toilet v
suitcase b	sheet l	towel t
form e	TV p	soap r
key c	remote control o	hairdryer s
key card h	wardrobe n	
bill i		
receipt g		

9.4
R=receptionist, G1=Guest 1, G2=Guest 2, G3=Guest 3, G4=Guest 4, G5=Guest 5, G6=Guest 6

Conversation 1
G1 Hello. Can I have some clean towels please?
R Certainly. Which room are you in?

Conversation 2
G2 Excuse me. I don't have a hairdryer.
R I'm sorry. There should be one in your room. Uhm … OK. I can get one for you.

Conversation 3
R How can I help?
G3 I have to leave early tomorrow morning. Can I pay my bill tonight?

Conversation 4
G4 Today is my last day at the hotel and I need to go into town.
R OK.
G4 Can I leave my suitcase here at reception today?
R Yes, that's no problem at all.

Conversation 5
G5 The remote control doesn't work. Can I have a new one please?
R Yes, we'll get another one for you.

Conversation 6
G6 I'm very sorry. I can't find my key card. Can you replace it?
R Yes, we can. Don't worry. People lose their key cards all the time.

9.5
Conversation 1
A Mr Santos, would you like to visit our new production centre?
B Thank you. That would be interesting.

Conversation 2
A Ms Labbé, would you have dinner with me tomorrow evening?
B Thank you very much. I'd enjoy that.

Conversation 3
A Carla, I've got two tickets for a concert on Thursday. Would you like to come?
B Thanks for asking me, but I'm afraid I've got something planned.

Conversation 4
A Gianni, how about a trip to London on Saturday?
B I'd love to, but unfortunately I have to leave Saturday morning.

9.6
Conversation 1
A Hi, Bob. Are you busy this evening?
B No, why?
A How about playing tennis then?
B Great idea!

Conversation 2
A Renzo, what about coming to the football match with us on Sunday?
B Sorry, I can't. I'm going on holiday tomorrow.
A Oh, well, have a good holiday, then.

Conversation 3
A Michelle, why don't we go skiing on Sunday?
B I'd love to, but my mother's visiting us on Sunday. It's her birthday.

Conversation 4
A Lara, are you busy next Saturday?
B No, I don't think so.
A Let's go to the cinema.
B OK. Fine.

Unit 10
10.1
The North Face
Two hikers founded *The North Face* in San Francisco in 1966. They chose the company name because the 'north face' of a mountain is the most difficult to climb. Three years later the company began designing its own brand of climbing clothes and equipment, and in the 1980s the company started producing ski wear.

By 1989 *The North Face* offered a collection of outdoor wear, ski wear, sleeping bags, packs, and tents. In the mid-1990s *The North Face* designed more products for rock climbers, backpackers, and people who enjoy the outdoors. In spring 1999 it launched its own range of trekking and running shoes.

The North Face works with some amazing sportsmen and women. Dean Karnazes, who ran a marathon to the South Pole in running shoes in 2002, helps *The North Face* develop their running footwear and equipment.

10.2
P=Presenter, J=Jackie
P Have you ever bought a *North Face* product, Jackie?
J Yes, I've bought a jacket and a pair of their winter boots.
P And have you ever used these for hiking or climbing?
J No, I haven't. I've only used them for walks and going to town.
P I see. Actually, a lot of *North Face* customers these days are like you. They are not actually sports people. Originally, their products were for climbers and skiers. But their range of products has expanded a lot. For example, they have recently introduced a range of designer coats and jackets. Since 1969 they have also sponsored expeditions – the first one was to the Arctic. They have also sponsored a wide range of athletes like Kit DesLauriers who climbed Mount Everest and skied down from the summit.
J So the company has developed a lot since it started in 1966.
P That's right. But at the same time it has kept its original customers.

10.3
1 a I've finished the work.
   b I finished the work.
2 a He's solved the problem.
   b He solved the problem.

10.4
1 We've travelled a lot.
2 He changed his job.
3 I've corrected the mistake.
4 They've invited us to dinner.
5 I found my passport.
6 It's stopped raining.

10.5
1 a We've travelled a lot.
   b We travelled a lot.
2 a He's changed his job.
   b He changed his job.
3 a I've corrected the mistake.
   b I corrected the mistake.
4 a They've invited us to dinner.
   b They invited us to dinner.
5 a I've found my passport.
   b I found my passport.
6 a It's stopped raining.
   b It stopped raining.

10.6
T=Tom, J=Judith, L=Lara, F=Frank, P=Paul, S=Sue, D=Diane, K=Katie

Conversation 1
T My daughter's sick. I have to stay at home to look after her. She's only three.
J Fine. No problem.

Conversation 2
L What's Harry's phone number?
F I don't know. I'll look it up in the phone book.

Conversation 3
P I've lost an important piece of paper.
S Don't panic. I'll help you look for it.

Conversation 4
D Have you looked at the photos I sent you yet?
K Yes. I have. They are perfect for the company magazine.

10.7
1
Thank you for calling Airline Network. All our agents are busy at the moment. Please hold, and an agent will answer your call as soon as possible.
2
The office is now closed. We are open from 9.30 a.m. to 6.45 p.m., Monday to Saturday. Please call back during these times. In an emergency, please call 0118 956 7073.
3
The number you are dialling has changed. Please dial again, putting 0207 before the last seven digits.
4
This is Bob Steele's office. I'm sorry I can't take your call right now but please leave your name and number and I'll get back to you as soon as possible.
5
This is the Office World catalogue line. To receive our catalogue, please leave your name, address and postcode, spelling any difficult words. Thank you for your call.

10.8
T=Tonia, M= Max
T Max, it's Tonia.
M Sorry, who? It's a bad line.
T Max, it's Tonia. I've got a problem. I've just arrived. My plane was late. I'm very sorry but I don't think I'll be able to ...
M Hello ... hello? Tonia?
T Max, are you there?
M Yes. I'm on my mobile. We lost the connection.
T Yes. Look, Max, as I said, my plane was late and I'm still at the airport so I won't get to your office for 3.30.
M Don't worry. When can you get here?
T Er, in about an hour?
M OK. I'll tell the others. We'll wait till you arrive.
T Are you sure? Thanks a lot, Max. Bye.

10.9
H=Hans, D=Don
H Hello, Don, it's Hans. Am I disturbing you?
D Er ... I'm in a restaurant with a customer at the moment, but we're getting ready to leave. Could you call me back in about five minutes?
H Yes, of course.
(Later)
H Don, Hans again. Is it OK to talk now?
D Yeah, sorry I couldn't talk before. So you've arrived?
H At last! It's a long trip. Oh, Don, can you hold on a minute ... (Are you sure this is the right address?) Yes, yes, that's the right address ... Sorry about that Don, the taxi driver wanted to check the address. Right, can we fix a time to meet?
D Sure. Tomorrow's best for me. How about coming to my office around 12, then we have lunch together after?
H Good idea. See you at 12 tomorrow then.
D Yeah. Enjoy your first day in Chicago, Hans. Bye.

Answer key

Unit 1
Language focus p.6
1
Country: Belgium
Married/Single: Married
Children: Two

3
1 are you
2 do you
3 do you
4 company
5 Are you

4 Timo
6.30 (six thirty)
train
7.30 (seven thirty)
7.00 (seven o'clock)
8.00 (eight o'clock)

5 Stephanie
8.00 (eight)
bike
about 8.40 (eight forty)
3.00 (three)
4.00 (four)

Yes, I do.

Practice p.8
1
2 What time do you leave home?
3 How do you go to work?
4 What time do you get to work?
5 What time do you finish work?
6 What time do you get home?

4

At work	Stephanie	Timo
I read and write emails.	✓	✓
I read financial newspapers.		✓
I look at information on the Internet.		✓
I make phone calls.	✓	✓
I have meetings with clients and customers.	✓	✓
I give advice/information.	✓	
I have meetings with colleagues.	✓	✓
I have business lunches.		✓
I travel to other cities/countries.		✓

6 Stephanie says understanding English on the phone is difficult. Timo says spelling in English is difficult.

Wordpower p.10
1
2 repeat
3 Excuse, say
4 speak
5 say
6 write
7 borrow
8 mean
10 understand

2
1 c
2 a
3 b

3
a a folder
b a laptop
c a whiteboard
d a notebook
e a dictionary
f a pen
g an eraser
h a paper clip
i a pencil
j a hole punch
k a piece of paper

4
1 Yes. They can use the whiteboard in Dirk's office.
2 No. They play the CD on William's computer.

8
1 d
2 b
3 c
4 a

Focus on communication p.12
Introductions
2 1 a 2 c 3 b
3
2 this is
3 Pleased to meet you, too
4 Can I introduce
5 My name
6 do you know
7 this is
8 Hello
9 Nice to meet you

Greetings and goodbyes
1 1 c 2 d 3 a 4 b
2 a 1 b 3

3
Greetings
Good morning.
Hello …
It's good to see you again.
It's nice to be here again.
How are you?
Very well, thanks. And you?
How's the family?
Fine, thanks.
How's everything … ?

Goodbyes
It was nice meeting you.
I enjoyed meeting you, too.
It was great seeing you.
Have a good trip.
I hope to see you again soon.
See you again soon.
Goodbye.
Bye.

Unit 2
Language focus 1 p.14
1
1 Three hours.
2 By bus and train.
3 No, he doesn't. He has only fifteen or twenty minutes.

1 She starts work at 8.30.
2 He doesn't live here.
3 Does it arrive every day?

Pronunciation p.15
/s/ starts   /z/ lives   /ɪz/ finishes

Practice p.15
1
1 lives
2 works
3 develops
4 goes
5 starts
6 doesn't have
7 eats
8 works
9 doesn't go out
10 is
11 paints
12 has

2
2 Does she live in Hamburg?
3 Does she work for a bank?
4 How does she go to work?
5 What time does she start work?
6 What does she eat for lunch?
7 Does she go out a lot in the evenings?
8 What does she paint?
9 Where does she have exhibitions?

Language focus 2 p.16
1

Evening/weekend activities	Stephanie	Timo
watch TV		✓
relax		✓
go shopping	✓	
read	✓	
play the guitar		✓
go cycling	✓	
go swimming		✓
go skiing		✓
invite friends	✓	
have parties	✓	

We put adverbs of frequency before the verb, but after the verb *to be*.

Practice p.17

❸ travelling h
eating out a
swimming j
sightseeing c
shopping f
skiing e
walking/trekking i
going to clubs b
sunbathing/relaxing on a beach d
camping g

❺ (Possible answer)
He enjoys travelling to new places, walking, and trekking. He doesn't enjoy doing nothing or lying on a beach.

❻ We use the *-ing* form of the verb.

Wordpower p.18

❷ 1 14
2 60
3 70
4 18

❹ 2 24
3 16
4 55
5 97
6 72

❽ 8.30 eighty thirty or half past eight
3.15 three fifteen or quarter past three
7.50 seven fifty or ten to eight
7 seven o'clock
11.20 eleven twenty or twenty past eleven
3.05 three oh five or five past three
8.40 eight forty or twenty to nine
9.45 nine forty-five or quarter to ten

Focus on communication p.20
Starting a call

❷, ❸
6 Yes, speaking.
1 Good morning. L. S. Communications. How can I help you?
5 Hello. Is that Anna Pilon?
7 This is Mario Bardo. I'm calling about ...
2 Good morning. Can I speak to Anna Pilon, please?
4 Hello.
3 Just a moment, please.

❺ 2 Just a moment, please.   5 This is
3 Is that   6 I'm calling
4 Yes, speaking.

❼ 2 b   3 e   4 a   5 f   6 c

❽ Could I speak to ...?
Hold on, please.
I'm phoning about ...

Time expressions

❶ 1 at 4 p.m., on Tuesday, in the afternoon, at midday
2 next Monday, on Tuesday afternoon, at 3 o'clock
3 last week, yesterday evening, tomorrow morning

❷ **at** 4 p.m., midday, 3 o'clock
on Tuesday, Tuesday afternoon
in the afternoon
no preposition: next Monday, last week, yesterday evening, tomorrow morning

❸ 1 no preposition   4 in
2 on   5 no preposition
3 at   6 at

Review Unit A

❶ 1 speaks   5 travels   8 goes
2 are   6 visits   9 is
3 communicate   7 does   10 works
4 uses

❷ 1 Where do they live?
2 Who does he work for?
3 Does she go to work by car?
4 What time do you start work?
5 What does she do in her job?
6 Do you use English at work?

❸ have time
write emails
visit clients
go shopping
watch TV
speak English on the phone
read newspapers/emails

❻ 9.15 nine fifteen or a quarter past nine
10.30 ten thirty or half past ten
2.45 two forty-five or quarter to three
6.50 six fifty or ten to seven

❼ (Possible answers)
1 Pleased to meet you, too.
2 Nice to meet you, too.
3 It's good/nice to see you/to be here again.
4 Fine, thanks.
5 Very well, thanks, and you?
6 Fine, thanks./Very well, thanks.
7 I enjoyed meeting you, too.
8 Thank you./Thanks.

❽ (Possible answers)
1 can I help   4 Hold   7 This is
2 Can/Could I speak 5 that   8 phoning/calling
3 calling   6 speaking

❾

at	on	in	no preposition
10.30 a.m.	Wednesday	the afternoon	next Saturday
the weekend	Tuesday evening	the evening	last weekend
4 o'clock	Sunday morning	the morning	next year
			yesterday morning

Unit 3
Language focus p.24

❶ 1 f   5 a
2 e   6 c
3 d
4 b

❸

computer	✓
keyboard	✓
mouse	✓
printer	✗
phone	✗
pens	✓
paper	✓
diary	✗
calendar	✓
pictures on the walls	✗

❹

		true	false
1	There isn't a canteen in the office.	✓	
2	There is a coffee machine upstairs.		✓
3	There aren't any rooms with air conditioning.		✓
4	There is a car park in the next street.	✓	
5	There is one parking space in the office.	✓	

Use *there is/there's* with singular nouns.
Use *there are* with plural nouns.
Use *some* with plural nouns in positive sentences, where we don't say the number.
Use *any* with plural nouns in negative sentences and questions.

104 ● ANSWER KEY

Wordpower p.28

1
1 café
2 post office
3 department store
4 theatre
5 bookshop
6 chairs and tables
7 tourist information office
8 seafront

4
1 where is
2 is there, near here
3 Excuse me, looking for

5 Conversation 1: Thank you.
Conversation 2: Thanks. Thanks very much.
Conversation 3: Thanks.

Focus on communication p.30

Asking for and giving directions

1
a traffic lights   d square
b crossroads   e bridge
c pedestrian crossing

Asking for travel information

1
2 platform   5 return ticket
3 bus stop   6 receipt
4 single ticket

2

	train	bus	taxi		train	bus	taxi
1	✓	✓	✓	5			✓
2	✓		✓	6		✓	
3	✓			7	✓		✓
4		✓		8			✓

3
Destination   Victoria
Ticket   Single
Fare   £17.50
Next train   at five thirty, in eleven minutes
Platform   2
Journey time forty-five minutes

Unit 4

Language focus 1 p.32

2
1 A travel book company.
2 No, they also publish maps and phrasebooks.
3 Digital guides.

3
1 Cheap, independent adventure travel.
2 There weren't any books about budget travel.
3 *Lonely Planet*.

> Yes, the Past Simple is the same for all persons.
> He didn't work.
> She didn't study.

Practice p.33

1 lived, wanted, asked, followed, decided, borrowed, worked, finished, liked, showed, invited

Pronunciation p.33

/d/	/t/	/ɪd/
borrowed	asked	decided
followed	finished	invited
lived	liked	wanted
showed	worked	
travelled		

2 bought, left, went, saw, ate, took, wrote, began

3
2 lived
3 travelled
4 went
5 studied
6 got
7 worked
8 met
9 married

4
1 Tony didn't work for Chrysler for a long time.
2 He didn't meet his wife, Maureen, in Sydney.
3 They didn't travel to Australia by plane.
5 Maureen didn't buy a typewriter.

Language focus 2 p.34

1
1 Because they wanted to make a long journey before they returned to London.
2 In their very small flat in Sydney.
3 $1,200.

> 1 Did he return yesterday?
> 2 Did they go to the USA?

Practice p.35

1
1 a arrive
  b lose
  c take
  d leave
  e break
  f wake up

2 a He woke up late.
  b He arrived late.
  c He lost his luggage.
  d He left his laptop in a taxi.
  e He took the wrong train.
  f He broke his leg.

2
2 When/Why
3 What
4 When/Why
5 Did
6 Did
7 What
8 Did

Wordpower p.36

1 Weather: hot, wet, cloudy, sunny, cold
Method of travel: plane, ferry, train
Destinations: a hotel, a factory, Hong Kong, the USA

3 1 e   2 a   3 h   4 c   5 f   6 b   7 d   8 g

4 It was awful!, It wasn't very good., It was OK., It was good., It was very good., It was fabulous!

Focus on communication p.38

Leaving a message

1
3 One moment please. I'm sorry, the line's busy. Will you hold?
1 Good morning. Sava Electronics.
4 Er, no, I'll call again later. Thank you. Goodbye.
5 Goodbye.
2 Good morning. Can I have extension 473, please?

4
1 I'm sorry, the line's busy.
2 Will you hold?
3 I'll call again later.

6 2 c   3 b   4 e   5 a   6 g   7 f

Telephone numbers

2
a 0208-553-9057   c 75-30-6929
b 0143-4285611   d 001212-5315898

Spelling

1

(say)	(he)	(egg)	(eye)	(you)
/eɪ/	/iː/	/e/	/aɪ/	/uː/
j	d	n	y	u
k	e	x		

3 2 Italian   3 Polish   4 Spanish   5 Thai   6 Brazilian

Review Unit B

❶
1. museum
2. hotel
3. restaurant
4. chemist's
5. cinema
6. metro station

❸
1. Have you got
2. Have you got
3. Does she have
4. Do you have
5. Have they got
6. Does he have

❹
1. a sunny b windy c wet d cold e hot
2. a plane b ferry c train d car

❺
1. bought/didn't buy
2. ate/didn't eat
3. wrote/didn't write
4. went/didn't go
5. left/didn't leave
6. was/wasn't
7. met/didn't meet
8. studied/didn't study

❻ Conversation 1
1. extension
2. please
3. moment
4. sorry
5. busy/engaged
6. hold
7. call/ring
8. back/again
9. Goodbye
10. Goodbye

Conversation 2
1. sorry
2. take
3. message
4. Can/Could
5. call
6. name
7. is
8. number
9. can/could
10. say
11. spell
12. name
13. give
14. message

Unit 5

Language focus 1 p.42

❷
1. d 4. g 7. b
2. a 5. e
3. f 6. c

❸
1. 200 million people.
2. Better transportation, package holidays, the media.
3. Flights and accomodation.

❺
1. How much money *does* tourism make? $3.6 trillion
2. When *did* rail travel get better? In the 1840s.
3. How *do* travel companies use newspapers? To advertise their products.
4. What information *do* people get from the Internet? Travel information.

Practice

❶
1. count, mass
2. count, mass
3. mass, mass, mass
4. count, mass, count
5. mass, mass, count, count

❷
1. –
2. newspapers
3. –
4. tourists
5. –
6. –

Language focus 2 p.44

❸
1. 1950
2. 1970
3. 1990
4. 2000
5. 2020

❹
1. b
2. d
3. c
4. a

❺ c

❻
1. $1,000
2. $400
3. $140
4. $1.34

Use *some* and *a lot of* with both mass and count nouns in positive sentences.
Use *many* with count nouns in negative sentences and in questions.
Use *much* with mass nouns in negative sentences and in questions.

Practice p.45

❶
1. How many tourists were there in 1970? 166 million; How many tourists were there in 1990? 458 million.; How many tourists were there in 2000? 698 million; How many tourists will there be in 2020? 1.5 billion.

❷ How much does a visitor to France spend? $400; What is the income for the local people? $140; What was the total income for Costa Rica last year? $1.34 billion.

❸
2. How much money did you spend?
3. How many days did you stay?
4. How many places did you visit?
5. How much luggage did you take?
6. How many problems did you have?
7. How much food did you eat?
8. How many wild animals did you see?

Wordpower p.46

❶
apples a	chocolate cake o	orange juice k
bananas b	fish f	potatoes q
beef g	ice cream p	strawberries c
beer h	milk m	tomatoes v
broccoli u	mineral water i	tea j
carrots r	mushrooms t	yogurt n
cheese l	onions s	
chicken e	oranges d	

Using a dictionary

❶
a. a count noun is shown with [C]
b. a mass or uncountable noun is shown with [U]

❷ C: apples, bananas, carrots, mushrooms, onions, oranges, potatoes, strawberries, tomatoes
M: beef, beer, broccoli, cheese, chicken, chocolate cake, fish, ice cream, milk, mineral water, orange juice, tea, yogurt

❸
a. a piece of advice
b. a bit/piece of information
c. a piece of luggage

Focus on communication p.48

❶ 1 No. 2 Two coffees.

❷ 2 d 3 f 4 c/e 5 a 6 c/e

❺ tomato and carrot soup, salmon pâté, chicken casserole, omelette, vegetables, side salad, glass of white wine, beer, still mineral water

❻ What would you like …? I'll have …
Would you like …? I'd like …
Could you …?

Unit 6

Language focus 1 p.50

❷

		true	false
1	The plane from Sydney to Perth is more expensive than the train.		✓
2	There are fewer trains than flights between Sydney and Perth.	✓	
3	Trains are more harmful to the environment than planes.		✓
4	Travelling by train across Australia is more boring than flying.		✓
5	Martina thinks taking the train is better than flying.	✓	

cheaper, slower, fewer, bigger, happier, more frequent, more expensive, more harmful, more boring
The consonant doubles.

Practice p.51

1
1 Yes.
2 No. She was with a friend.
3 Mountain biking. (a)

2
2 more crowded
3 cleaner
4 more expensive
5 quieter
6 older
7 younger
8 more adventurous

4 (Possible answers)
1 quieter
2 cheaper
3 more exciting
4 more interesting
5 more dangerous

Language focus 2 p.52

Comparative adjectives: *cleaner, nicer, safer, friendlier, prettier, easier, more popular, more attractive, more fascinating, more interesting, better*
Superlative adjectives: *nicest, safest, prettiest, easiest, most attractive, most fascinating, most interesting, best*
Change the *–y* to *–i* and add *–est* to the end of the adjective.
Put *the most* before the adjective.

Practice p.53

1 Average $470
Paris $670
Madrid $550
Bangkok $340
São Paulo $290
Prague $270

2
1 highest
2 cheaper
3 higher
4 lower
5 more expensive
6 lowest

Wordpower p.54

Dates

1
1 the first of May/May the first
2 the second of April/April the second
3 the tenth of March/March the tenth
4 the nineteenth of August/August the nineteenth
5 the twenty-fourth of September/September the twenty-fourth

3
1 17th
2 30th
3 16th
4 12th

4 In the UK the order is day, month, year. In the USA the order is month, day, year.

Money

1
1 d
2 f
3 a
4 e
5 c
6 b

2 Conversation 1: c
Conversation 2: b
Conversation 3: a

3
1 note, notes, coins
2 cash, cash machine
3 credit, credit, debit

5
1 earn
2 on
3 in, by
4 receipts
5 with

Focus on communication p.56

2
	Conversation 1	Conversation 2
the visitor's journey	✓	✓
the visit	✓	✓
home town/country	✓	
work	✓	
travel and holidays	✓	✓
accommodation		✓

3 Do you come from ... (*Dublin*)?
Do you live in ... (*Barcelona*)?
Is this your first visit to ... (*Dublin*)?
Do you travel a lot for work?
Where do you work?

4, 5
1 Did you have a good trip? (the visitor's journey)
2 Is it your first time in New York? (the visit)
3 How long are you here for? (the visit)
4 Do you travel abroad much? (travel and holidays)
5 Do you enjoy travelling? (travel and holidays)
6 Is everything at the hotel OK? (accommodation)

Review Unit C

1
newspaper C	traffic M	tomato C
transportation M	banana C	work M
travel M	money M	apple C
company C	industry C	luggage M
information M	plane C	tourist C
potato C	wine M	

2
1 many
2 a lot of
3 much/a lot of
4 a lot of
5 much
6 many/a lot of
7 much/a lot of

3
		Comparative	Superlative
1	few	fewer	fewest
2	quick	quicker	quickest
3	easy	easier	easiest
4	dangerous	more dangerous	most dangerous
5	crowded	more crowded	most crowded
6	happy	happier	happiest
7	big	bigger	biggest
8	good	better	best
9	bad	worse	worst
10	friendly	friendlier	friendliest
11	expensive	more expensive	most expensive
12	clean	cleaner	cleanest

4 British English
1 the ninth of January nineteen ninety-nine
2 the twelfth of March two thousand
3 the eleventh of April two thousand and two/twenty oh two
4 the seventh of August nineteen ninety
5 The second of October nineteen seventy-two

American English
1 September first nineteen ninety-nine
2 December third two thousand
3 November fourth two thousand and two/twenty oh two
4 July eighth nineteen ninety
5 February tenth nineteen seventy-two

5
1 a a note
b a cash machine
c a credit card
d coins
2 a I spent $200 on food when I was at the conference.
b Most workers in this country earn more than $1,000 a month.
c After you get a taxi, always get a receipt from the driver.
d I don't have my credit card so I have to pay in cash.
e I paid for my flight by credit card.

Unit 7

Language focus 1 p.60

❶ 1 c
2 d
3 a
4 b

❷ 1 She writes about the USA, mainly about politics and business.
2 She writes for two newspapers and a business magazine.

❸ 1 She is writing about the US election.
2 She is preparing a special report on the US computer industry.

Practice p.61

❶ 1 R
2 C
3 R
4 C
5 C
6 R

❷ Present Simple: 1, 3, 6
Present Continuous: 2, 4, 5

❸ 1 c
2 d
3 a
4 b

❹ regular activity: 1, 3
current activity: 2, 4

Pronunciation p.61

❷ 1 He isn't working here.
2 You aren't winning the game.
3 We aren't going on holiday.
4 I'm not listening to the radio.
5 She isn't helping them.
6 They aren't playing football.

Language focus 2 p.62

❶ 1 c
2 e
3 b
4 a
5 d

❸ 1 40% of US workers.
2 They are too busy or they forget.
3 No.

> **Present trends**
> US workers are taking fewer holidays this year.
> People are also having shorter holidays than before.
> In the USA the situation is becoming serious.
> Workers are damaging their health.
> We use Present Continuous to talk about a present trend.
>
> **Other examples in the article**
> US workers ... are working harder than before.
> 40% of US workers are not going on holiday...
> ... why are workers not going on holiday?
> ... companies are encouraging their employees to leave the office more.

Wordpower p.64

❶ (Possible answer) He has a lot of work. He doesn't have much time. He has a lot of stress.

❷ 1 12
2 7 a.m.
3 visit customers
4 get to meetings on time
5 usually, sometimes by taxi
6 swimming

❸ make an arrangement, make a plan

❹ make: appointments, a change, a decision, a mistake
do: business, my best, overtime, shopping, housework, sport
get: emails, home, to meetings, a taxi, the train

❺ 1 get to work, get home, get to meetings
2 get emails
3 get a taxi, get the train

Focus on communication p.66

❶ 2 13 August   4 11 August
3 10 August   5 19 August

❷ 1 She's phoning to arrange a meeting.
2 At 2.30 on Thursday afternoon.

❸ Is ... possible for you?   ... is OK.
What about ... ?   Yes, that's fine.
How about ... ?   No, I'm sorry, I'm busy on ...
See you on ... , then.   No, ... isn't possible.

❹ 1 are they staying   2 I'm visiting   3 They're going

❺ 1 They're talking about activities happening in the future.
2 When we talk about fixed arrangements.

❽ 1 She's phoning him to change the appointment.
2 They arrange to meet at 3.15 on Monday afternoon.

❾ 1 Can we change   4 do you prefer
2 When are you free?   5 that's fine
3 not possible for me 6 See you

Unit 8

Language focus 1 p.68

❶ South Korea Quiz
1 a
2 c
3 b
4 b
5 c

Poland Quiz
1 c
2 c
3 a
4 b
5 a

❷ 1 Warsaw.
2 His company asked him to move to their head office in Seoul.
3 He needs some advice about life in Korea.

❸ 1 c
2 e
3 d
4 a
5 b

❺ Predictions: maybe he will need to be a little careful, They will ask ... , It will be great. He will love it ..., he will probably go out to bars and restaurants with his colleagues, No, it won't.
We use *will* to predict future situations.

Practice p.69

❶ 1 will be
2 'll snow
3 'll need
4 will, speak
5 won't have

Language focus 2 p.70

❶ 1 He is going to learn about life in Korea.
2 He sits next to Karol at the office.
3 Karol and Dong-gun are going to look at apartments.
4 No. He is going to go to Busan for work.
5 He is going to start learning Korean.

❷ Karol's future plans: I'm going to learn about life in Korea. Dong-gun and I are going to look at some apartments. In the evening he's going to take me to a restaurant to try Korean food for the first time. Next week I'm going to visit our local office in Busan. I'm going to start a (Korean) course on September 4th.
He uses the *going to* future for his future plans.

Practice p.71

❶ 1 They are going to speak to the local staff in the Busan office.
2 They are going to have breakfast at the hotel.
3 They are going to go to the factory.
4 They are going to give presentations.
5 They are going to meet the regional manager.
6 They are going to talk to the international sales team.

Wordpower p.72

1
- address c
- envelope a
- postcode/zip code d
- stamp b
- fax machine f
- mobile/cellphone e
- phone with answerphone g
- attachment i
- CD-ROM r
- desktop PC m
- disk drive n
- email address h
- keyboard l
- laptop j
- monitor k
- mouse p
- USB port o
- printer q

6
1. www.cnn.com
2. www.healthnet.org.uk
3. russelg@clara.net
4. p.pezzini@rol.com
5. roychapman@altavista.net

Focus on communication p.74

2 1 d 2 c 3 b 4 e 5 a

3
Starting
Thank you for your fax (*of 29 January*)
Thanks for your email
Saying why you're writing
This fax is (*to confirm your visit ...*)
This email is (*to get in touch again*)
Requesting
Could you please email me (*details of ...*)
Please let me know (*if there's a problem ...*)
Giving bad news
I am sorry (*to inform you ...*)
Apologizing
I apologize for (*the change of plans*)
Ending
Please contact us again (*if you would like further information*)
Looking forward to (*meeting you next week*)
Hoping (*to see you soon*)

Review Unit D

1
1. works
2. are visiting
3. is going up
4. start
5. do, live
6. are not taking

3 (Possible answers)
I'm going to ask Bob about his plans for the Asia sales team.
I'm going to phone Tokyo office to arrange my visit for next month.
I'm going to buy souvenirs for my Japanese customers.
I'm going to learn some phrases to introduce myself in Japanese.
I'm going to get some guide books and plan a trip for my day off.

4 do: homework, the shopping, the housework, a sport, some work, business (with someone)
make: a mistake, a business trip, a decision, an appointment, a phone call, a change

5
Conversation 1	Conversation 2
1 is that	1 It's
2 speaking	2 sorry
3 calling/phoning	3 Can/Could
4 you free	4 change
5 sorry	5 free
6 about	6 OK/possible
7 possible	7 about
8 fine/OK	8 fine
9 say	9 See you
	10 Thanks

6 1 1 b/d 2 f 3 a 4 i 5 h 6 c 7 b/d 8 j 9 e 10 g
2 Starting 1, 7
Saying why you're writing 5, 9
Requesting 2, 4
Giving bad news 10
Apologizing 6
Ending 3, 8

Unit 9

Language focus p.78

1 Prisons converted into hotels.

3
1. Malmaison is in Oxford, UK. Hostel Celica is in Ljubljana, Slovenia.
2. The governor's house.
3. The original cells.
4. The prison walls, and the windows and doors.
5. Music concerts and art exhibitions.

> Should: you should ask at reception, you shouldn't leave money or valuables in your room
> Can: you can also spend the night in the governor's house, you can't stay in these rooms, you can only look at them, you can't escape the hotel's history, guests can see graffiti on the prison walls
> Have to: businesses have to be innovative, you don't have to spend a lot of money
> We put *should* and *can* before the subject, e.g. *Should/Can I go?*
> We use *do, does,* or *did* and change the position of the subject and verb, e.g. *Do I have to go?*

Pronunciation p.79

2
1 a   5 b
2 b   6 b
3 a   7 a
4 a   8 b

Practice p.80

1
1. can
2. shouldn't
3. don't have to, can
4. should
5. have to, can't

Wordpower p.82

1 1 Reception
- lift (BrE)/elevator (AmE) f
- stairs d
- luggage a
- suitcase b
- form (= hotel registration form) e
- key c
- key card h
- bill i
- receipt g

Bedroom
- blanket k
- hangers m
- pillow j
- sheet l
- TV p
- remote control o
- wardrobe n

Bathroom
- bath u
- shower q
- toilet v
- towel t
- soap r
- hairdryer s

4
1 c
2 e
3 b
4 f
5 a
6 d

5
1. The guest wants some clean towels.
2. The guest wants a hairdryer.
3. The guest wants to pay the bill.
4. The guest wants to leave a suitcase at reception.
5. The guest wants a new remote control.
6. The guest wants a new key card.

6 "They're too heavy to carry." suitcases
"I need it to show to my boss because my company is paying for the hotel." a receipt/the hotel bill
"There are only two in the wardrobe and we have lots of clothes." hangers
"It's cold today. I need another one on my bed." a blanket
"I don't have time for one. I'll have a shower instead." a bath
"I put it in the lock, but it doesn't work." the key
"He doesn't want to walk up them, because he has to carry his suitcases." the stairs
"I always sleep with two under my head, but the bed only has one." pillows
"Every guest has to complete this when they check into the hotel." form/hotel registration form

Focus on communication p.84
Invitations
1 Conversation Picture
1 c
2 a
3 d
4 b

2 Would you like to (*visit* ...)? — Thank you. That would be interesting.
Would you have (*dinner*) with me ...? — Thank you very much. I'd enjoy that.
How about (*a trip to* ...)? — Thanks for asking me, but I'm afraid (*I've got* ...)
I'd love to, but unfortunately (*I have to* ...)

Suggestions
1 1 Bob Yes 2 Renzo No 3 Michelle No 4 Lara Yes
2 How about (*playing* ...)? — Great idea.
What about (*coming* ...)? — OK. Fine.
Why don't we (*go* ...)? — Sorry, I can't. (*I'm going* ...).
Let's (go ...). — I'd love to, but (*my mother* ...).

Unit 10
Language focus p.86
1 a mountain climbing
b skiing
c snowboarding
d hiking
e long-distance running

2 The North Face
Two hikers founded *The North Face* in **San Francisco** in 1966. They chose the company name because the 'north face' of a mountain is the **most difficult** to climb. Three years later the company began designing its own brand of climbing clothes and equipment, and in the 1980s the company started producing **ski wear**.
By 1989 *The North Face* offered a collection of outdoor wear, ski wear, sleeping bags, packs, and tents. In **the mid-1990s** *The North Face* designed more products for rock climbers, backpackers, and people who enjoy the outdoors. In spring 1999 it started its own range of trekking and running shoes.
The North Face works with some amazing sportsmen and women. Dean Karnazes, who ran a marathon to the **South Pole** in running shoes in 2002, helps *The North Face* develop their running footwear and equipment.
3 1 c 2 d 3 e 4 b 5 a
4 1 climbers, skiers
2 coats, jackets
3 expeditions
4 Mount Everest, skied
5 original customers

Pronunciation p.88
2 1 a 2 b 3 a 4 a 5 b 6 a

Practice p.88
1 1 They had a long holiday last year.
2 Correct.
3 Did you live in Madrid in 2005?
4 Correct.
5 Correct.
6 He started a new job a month ago.
7 I phoned you three times yesterday.

2 1 has had
2 has opened
3 expanded
4 sponsored
5 has advertised
6 launched

3

Infinitive	Past Simple	Past Participle
fly	flew	flown
forget	forgot	forgotten
have	had	had
lose	lost	lost
win	won	won

Wordpower p.90
1 2 apologize for a mistake
3 put on a jacket
4 go for a walk
5 wait for a bus
6 pay for a ticket
7 turn on a TV
8 thank someone for help
9 get on a train
10 go on holiday
2 1 after
2 up
3 for
4 at

Focus on communication p.92
Answerphone messages
1 a 3 c 2 d 5 e 4
2 Call 1 calling, busy, hold, will answer
Call 2 9.30 a.m., 6.45 p.m., call back, 7073
Call 3 has changed, 0207, seven
Call 4 your call, name, number, get back
Call 5 receive, address, words, your call

Emails and mobile phones
1 (Possible answer) Emails are usually shorter, more informal, arrive immediately, and the sender usually expects a quick response.
2 1 Tonia is calling Max to tell him she won't get to his office for 3.30 because her plane arrived late.
2 At an airport.
3 She loses the connection and has to call again.
3 (Possible answer) The use of first names. It begins *Hi Hans* and ends *Best regards Don*.
4 1 Hans and Don.
2 (Possible answer) Yes, they are. Don answers Hans' first call when he's in a restaurant. Hans makes his second call when he's in a taxi.
5 1 Could you call me back
2 Is it OK to talk now
3 sorry I couldn't talk
4 can you hold on a minute
5 Sorry about that
6 How about coming
7 See you at 12
6 a 1, 2, 3, 5 b 4, 6, 7

Review Unit E
1 1 have to
2 don't have to
3 should
4 can
5 shouldn't
6 can't
2 1 Have you ever lived in another country?
Where did you live?
When did you live there?
2 Have you ever broken a bone?
What did you break?
How did you break it?
3 Have you ever won a prize?
What did you win?
When did you win it?

3
1. spent
2. did you visit
3. has travelled
4. have you travelled
5. Did they arrive
6. has increased
7. were
8. have opened

4
1. for
2. on/up
3. up
4. on
5. for
6. for
7. on
8. for

5
1. suitcase
2. stairs
3. lift (UK) elevator (US)
4. soap
5. towel
6. bill
7. receipt
8. key, key card

6 (Possible answers)

Conversation 1
A would you like to
B would be interesting

Conversation 2
A How/What about
B love to

Conversation 3
A would you like to
B enjoy that

Conversation 4
A How/What about
B that's a good idea

Conversation 5
A don't we
B sorry

Conversation 6
A why don't we
B a good idea

7 (Possible answers)
1. Sorry, we lost the connection.
2. Am I disturbing you?/Am I interrupting anything?/Is this a good time to call?
3. The line's breaking up./I can't hear you. Can you hang up and I'll call you again?
4. I think my mobile needs recharging.